# The TRUE(ish) HISTORY OF IRELAND

# The TRUE(ISH) HISTORY OF IRELAND

**Garvan Grant**
**Illustrated by Gerard Crowley**

MERCIER PRESS
IRISH PUBLISHER – IRISH STORY

**FOR DOMINI, LAUREN, MAEVE –
AND THE OTHER MAEVE. GG**

MERCIER PRESS

Cork

www.mercierpress.ie

© Text: Garvan Grant, 2015

© Illustrations: Gerard Crowley, 2015

ISBN: 978 1 78117 273 5

10 9 8 7 6 5 4 3 2 1

Printed and bound in the EU.

# CONTENTS

# INTRODUCTION

*History, it's a funny old game.*
Oscar Wilde (attrib.)

**Did you ever think there was something funny about Irish history?**
**Well, it turns out you were right.**

They say history is written by the victors, yet the Irish only really started being victorious after 1916. This means a lot of dodgy stuff was written about Ireland by other people for hundreds of years before then. Now it's time for us to put the record straight. Or straightish, at least. Using hearsay, rumour and some deadly cartoons, *The True(ish) History of Ireland* is an almost factual look at the birth, childhood and adolescence of an almost fully mature nation. Even better, it's told through the eyes of its proud, fun-loving natives.

From that fateful day thousands of years ago when a lovely northern European chap with long hair and a longer beard was stranded on the island, right up to late yesterday evening when the Irish were hard at work creating another never-ending boom, the book gets to the very heart of what it means to be a True Gael. It looks at the major events in the blessed history of this benighted isle, including the accidental invention of poitín by St Patrick, the conquest of the country by some rather posh English people and the discovery of the legendary Everlasting Pint in a cave in east Galway. It sums up the joyous, glorious and often hilarious experience of being Irish.

As well as providing readers with twenty chapters containing some fascinating half-truths about Irish history, we also tracked down a family that can trace its roots from 8,000 BCE right up to earlier this morning. Throughout history, various members of the Sweeney clan played a pivotal role in the formation of Ireland, so we profiled some of the better-known ones, though we also left out a few of the nastier ones.

And if that isn't enough, there are lists – lots and lots of lists. In fact, we were even thinking of doing a list of The Top Twenty Lists in *The True(ish) History of Ireland*, but decided that that might be pushing our luck. However, if you want to know what the top five rainiest rains in Ireland are (see page 30) or what Ireland's most useful inventions have been (see page 60), then read on!

Sometimes, historians have to make stuff up to fill in the gaps. This is no less true of *The True(ish) History of Ireland*, where many facts have been changed to protect the innocent. (Note: when the authors were paid, we've also protected the guilty.) So, as you read this book, remember that history is not always true. Much of it is merely true*ish*.

But the most important thing about reading *The True(ish) History of Ireland* is to enjoy it and not take it too seriously. If you do spot any errors you can send them to Brian Boru, c/o The Distant Past, Somewhere Near Dublin.

Thanks for reading,
Garvan and Gerard.

# 1

# BEFORE THERE EVEN WAS HISTORY

**Island for Sale or Rent**

As ridiculous as it may sound now, there was a time when not even Irish people lived in Ireland. The island was even described as 'a bit uninhabitable' in the first edition of *Island Monthly*, the glossy prehistoric magazine targeted at the world's wealthiest island-buyers. A copy of the magazine was discovered recently by archaeologists digging in north Offaly.

Prior to prehistoric times, the island, which didn't become known as Ireland until a few years later, was even attached to Britain, France and the rest of mainland Europe. It is still not clear what caused it to detach and drift away, although some French people claim they were only trying to get rid of the English, whom they traditionally love to hate. 'We must have pushed too hard,' a spokesman for France said at the time, though probably in a fairly strong French accent.

**Ever so Slightly Boring**

As you can imagine, being uninhabited can be a pretty tedious existence for an island, particularly if the eventual natives would go on to become some of the most fun-loving people in the whole of Europe. As there was no one living in Ireland, there were also no pubs, no parties and very few sing-alongs. On the plus side, there were no hangovers, no fighting and very few sing-alongs.

Although we have practically no photographs of Ireland back then, it is safe to say that it was a wet, stormy and rather dark place, particularly during the winter, which would often last for twelve months or more each year. Apart from the wind blowing and the odd shower, very little happened. That is not to say that there wasn't some excitement, particularly when the sun rose every morning, took one look at the mass of grey clouds and then just kind of sat there wondering what to do for the day. Later, it would get bored and sort of fall slowly out of the sky, letting the darkness take over again.

**Life: the Early Years**

Naturally, this is a very human-centred view of Ireland. But fossil records, carbon dating and articles in glossy nature magazines reveal that the island was teeming with life even before humans decided that living there might be a workable plan.

**Dinosaurs inhabited the country a few years before humans.**

Some of the earliest animals that were indigenous to the island and enjoyed its primordial ooze included the common-or-garden amoeba, the coelacanth and the sheep. Later, it is believed that a bunch of dinosaurs moved to Ireland from northern France. This group included a Tyrannosaurus rex, two Diplodocuses, a

Paddyosaurus and a Mickosaurus. (Note: the last two mentioned may have been made up in the twelfth century by mischievous Irish palaeontologists, many of whom were notorious pranksters.) These first dinosaurs are believed to have only stayed in Ireland for about two weeks as, even though they were notoriously cold-blooded, the climate just didn't do it for them; either that or they only came on a two-week holiday in the first place. Some of their hardier cousins did come back to live in Ireland later, though they brought lots of warm clothes and umbrellas with them.

### Survival of the Irishest

It is not clear how much the later dinosaur arrivals liked their new home as there are very few, if any left to ask these days. They were probably booted out by the notoriously aggressive goats and sheep living on the island (or were wiped out by a very large asteroid about 66 million years ago). This meant that other animals thrived as they didn't get eaten by dinosaurs, though the Irish duck-billed platypus who, by all accounts, wasn't particularly tasty, probably would have survived either way.

The animals that did well included goats, squirrels, wolfhounds, koalas, wombats, kangaroos and, of course, snakes. Most of these have survived to this day and still roam the countryside as if they own it, though Irish people are quick to point out that these animals have no legal claim on ownership of the land. Some of the animals above were deported to Australia, while the last-mentioned ones disappeared on a particularly dark day in the fifth century, which snakes still refer to as The Saint Patrick's Day Massacre.

**Prehistoric Ireland had a hard time even attracting tourists.**

## Wild, Wet and Wetter

Apart from the odd bit of rubbish that people on passing ships would toss overboard, Ireland was mainly covered in trees, rocks, grass and sheep. These all contributed towards making the island an unattractive proposition for human habitation. In time, however, Irish people learned to coexist peacefully with the trees, rocks and grass, though there are still some issues with the sheep. To this day, many have refused to vacate some of the higher, rockier and less habitable parts of the country, though negotiations with the state are ongoing.

The only other thing that was happy to live in Ireland before humans arrived was rain, which loved nothing more than falling all over the country for days – and often centuries – on end. Meteorological historians have actually found evidence that it poured every single day from 40 million BCE to 20 million BCE. Historians call this part of the country's history the Wet Ages, though most other parts of the island's history could also be described as the Wet Ages, except for medieval times, which are known as the Dark Wet Ages.

## Stranded Destiny

In many ways, the most attractive quality the island of Ireland had back in the day was that it was uninhabitable. If it had been particularly habitable, it must be presumed that people would already have been living there. However, Ireland's destiny was about to change when, one fateful day, a ship with a precious human cargo sailed into one of Ireland's 'black pools' (or 'dubh linn' in Irish, if there had been any Irish at the time). Were some 'foreigners' unwittingly about to become Irish? Only history would tell.

## Not Quite the Promised Land

Before the Irish inhabited Ireland, many Europeans were curious about the island, with some southern Europeans even using it as a potential holiday destination. They thought it would provide the chance to get away from the relentless sunshine and unending good weather they had to endure from April to September each year. However, very few actually thought it would be a good idea to live there.

Interestingly, the Bible contains the first ever reference in a historical document to Ireland. The *Book of Genesis* describes how Noah saved remnants of all the creatures of Earth from the flood, including, for some unfathomable reason, hippos, black widow spiders and gnats. It is written that God then centred the rising water in and around 'Irelandius', as it was a logical spot to have a flood.

Ireland is also believed to be the first land that Noah and his family spotted after sailing around for more than 150 days in the lashing rain, though this was just a drop in the ocean as far as Ireland was concerned. However, after taking a good look at the island from their ark and even letting some llamas off in The Barren (now The Burren) in Co. Clare, they decided it 'was land, but just not the right kind of land'. It was another seven years before the Ark came close to land again, though it is not recorded in the Bible if Noah regretted his decision not to begin his repopulation plans in the west of Ireland. If he had, the Irish might have been the Chosen Ones and Jesus Christ might eventually have been born in or near Roscommon.

# Top Five

## Non-Human Life Forms that Ruled Ireland

The history of any country often concentrates on the achievements – or lack thereof – of its human inhabitants, but it is crucial not to forget the contributions of the various other animals which have called a place home and often for a lot longer than any people could.

1) **Pterodactyls:** These giant dinosaur birds are said to have enjoyed living on Ireland's highest points, or basically anywhere above the clouds. They enjoyed eating goats, spinach, penguins and bananas, though the latter were in very short supply in Ireland at the time. Most pterodactyls emigrated before the hunter-gatherers arrived from Europe or else died from a fatal and demoralising lack of bananas.

2) **Penguins:** For some bizarre reason, penguins originally lived in and around the Mediterranean Sea. However, the warm climate, the German tourists and the over-dependence on olive oil didn't suit them, so they went to live on the island of Ireland, which was called Hibernia or 'the land of eternal winter'. When they got there, they were threatened

by the pterodactyls and decided to move to the South Pole.

3) **Goats:** For millions of years before the arrival of the first human settlers, a battle for supremacy raged on the island of Ireland between goats and sheep on one side and dinosaurs and snakes on the other. The details of what happened aren't clear, but the goats and sheep eventually won out. Unfortunately, this then led to the Great Ovine-Caprine Wars of the Neolithic Age, the scars of which are still carried by Irish goats and sheep to this very day. The goats still celebrate this every year at the Puck Fair in Killorglin, when one of them dresses up like a king and orders all nearby humans to kneel down and worship him.

4) **Hermits:** There is some evidence that before Ireland was inhabited, some very, very holy men – who strictly speaking were human – snuck onto the island in order to pray, suffer and get incredibly wet all in the name of God. Unfortunately, it seems that none of them stuck around very long, meaning they were either called to their just reward or went home and spent the rest of their lives indulging in various types of sin.

5) **Rocks:** No plant, animal or form of weather has meant as much to Ireland as the humble rock. Thought to

have colonised the island at around the time of the Big Bang, rocks were believed by many to be the single most powerful entity in the country. Even as recently as the late twentieth century, Irish people have respected rocks for their longevity and ability to live so comfortably in such a challenging climate. Rocks, on the other hand, have never bothered to comment on what they think of the Irish.

# 2
# A PLACE TO CALL HOME

**The first human in Ireland had limited options.**

## Power to the People

Despite the sheep and the continuing absence of good places to get a pint, some Europeans decided they would give living on the island of Ireland a go. They arrived just after 10.30 a.m. on a relatively sunny August morning some 10,000 years ago, so these people had no idea about some of the harsher elements of Ireland's climate.

It has been speculated that these early settlers thought they had reached New York city and that they could thus claim the entire United States of America for themselves, which would have been some coup, particularly back then. Other historians have argued that the first inhabitants of Ireland were sent there from Northern Europe after committing various crimes on the mainland, including throwing French fries at Goths, singing 'Olé Olé Olé Olé' at the top of their voices and 'acting Irish', though no historian has been brave enough to speculate as to what this actually means.

Despite Noah's historical flirtation with the west coast, it is interesting to note that religious historians have ruled out the possibility that the Garden of Eden was located in the area now occupied by Donegal. For a start, no snakes had ventured that far north and it had very few apple trees. Also, God would never have allowed Adam and Eve to wander around the county completely naked even if there was no one else around. It could get pretty nippy in Donegal even in Biblical times.

**Takeaway lamb was very popular in Early Ireland.**

### First Contact

The first inhabitants, who most likely landed in Wexford or Waterford during the Middle Stone Age, were European hunter-gatherer types. As they were undoubtedly very intrepid, they must have been thrilled to find a completely uninhabited island with so much hunting and gathering just waiting to be done. They would have immediately set about hunting some of the plentiful supplies of squirrels, turnips and sheep, though most of the sheep just kind of stood there and didn't really need to be hunted. As for gathering, they would mainly have targeted blackberries, chocolate chip cookies and some of the slower-moving plants, such as broccoli.

## Middle Age Versus New Age

While the Mesolithics were happily hunting and gathering to their heart's content, the last thing they expected was the arrival of the Neolithics with their sophisticated ways, fancy clothes and something hot they called 'fire'. They were noticeably less hairy, could walk pretty much upright and wore shades even at night. They also looked down on the primitive Mesolithic folk and would shake their heads patronisingly if they saw one of them pushing a square wheel down the street.

Being New Stone Age folk, they would have considered hunting and gathering to have been a bit passé and so set about capturing various animals and vegetables which they hoped to domesticate. They had a lot of success domesticating sheep, magpies and carrots, though they were less successful with tarantulas, velociraptors and some of the wilder varieties of spinach.

## Rooms, Tombs and Booms

The Neolithic people also collected things that were crucial for their survival in the punishing Irish winters, including big leaves, any rocks that hadn't yet been hunted or gathered and mud. Using stones that just happened to be shaped like handy tools, they then constructed their very own primitive dwellings (or 'houses', as other humans tended to call them).

Unfortunately, a lot of these 'houses' were quite shaky and would often fall down on top of whoever happened to be in them at the time. They thus ended up becoming tombs, which inadvertently led to a huge number of 'tombs' being constructed all over the island.

Indeed, such was the settlers' mastery of tomb-building that the Irish became the market leader in tombs from 4,000 BCE until 2,000 BCE. Historians refer to this period as the pre-Celtic Tiger economy. A few of these tombs are still standing, such as the one at Newgrange in Co. Meath; however, most of the rest of them aren't and often look like big piles of rocks to the untrained eye.

## Cool Celtic Conflict

If the Mesolithics thought the Neolithics were sophisticated, they were to get a real wake-up call when the next settlers arrived. The Celts, with their hair gel, fancy jewellery and extremely sharp weapons, were not popular in Europe as they liked nothing more than a good fight. This led to other Europeans chasing them across the continent until they ran out of land, which is why they ended up in Ireland.

While the Mesolithic and Neolithic peoples had lived together in relative harmony, the Celts were a lot more aggressive and loved to stir things up by declaring war on their neighbours every morning before breakfast. This led to the establishment of various warring factions, including the Stone Age Republican Army, the Neolithic Liberation Army and the Celtic Defenders Association. In the space of just a few thousand years, Ireland had gone from being a peaceful, uninhabited island to one of the most violent places on the planet. It is still not clear what caused this change, though many animals and plants blame the humans.

## The Painful Birth of a Nation

However, the fighting couldn't go on forever and a truce was eventually reached between the Mesolithic, Neolithic and Celtic peoples. At a famous summit in Tara, just before the turn of the millennium, they all agreed to stop fighting and become one nation. They also decided to drop the off-putting 'Hibernia' name, as an island that was called after the coldest season of the year was never going to attract tourists. Instead they went with Ireland, as it sounded quite like Our Land, which was really nice and inclusive.

It was a glorious day of unity for all the people of the island, who swore there and then that there would never again be the kind of silly infighting that had plagued the country for so long.

## Throwing the First Ever Landing Party

Obviously historians can never be sure what happened on that day some 10,000 years ago when the first human beings decided to step onto the island of Ireland – unless, of course, they read the account of the man who claims he took that historic step. His memoir was discovered in a bog in Sligo just a few weeks ago and should be available for examination and authentication in a couple of years.

Here is an extract from the autobiography of 'Sweeneyos', which has been translated from Mesolithic into modern English:

As our boat approached the shore, I asked the others: 'Really? There? You want to live there? It doesn't look like it's even possible. Please can we go back to France?' But they ignored me and pressed on.

The closer we got to land, the more scared I became. There were howls from deep within the island and trees clustered together on the cliffs as if they were trying to escape from something behind them. The only good thing was that it was relatively dry, windless and sunny, so if the climate stayed anything like this all year round, it might not be too bad.

When the boat was mere yards from land, the others pushed me out. I swam for the shore, clambered up and, for a moment, felt just a little special. I turned back to the people in the boat who were already sailing away and shouted, 'I hereby declare this to be my country. No person shall set foot here unless they have my permission'. But they were already out of earshot.

I then contemplated my position and thought I should probably get a flag together and write a national anthem. But there would be plenty of time for that. Today was a day of celebration, so I wandered inland to search for a town, a pub and maybe some ladies. Unfortunately, it was to be another two decades before these things finally made their way to my island.

And the rest is history.

# Top Five

## Rainiest Rains that Drench the Irish

There is a famous phrase about the weather in Ireland: 'If you can see the mountains, that means it's going to rain. If you can't see them, that means it is raining.' However, this suggests that there is only one type of rain in the country, whereas in fact there are nearly 3,000 different types afflicting Ireland on an annual basis.

1) **Soft rain:** Regardless of how light or heavy the rain actually is, 'soft rain' relates to how the person who says it is feeling. For example, if an Irish person has just finished confession, won the Lotto or had a very fine pint of stout, the rain is said to be 'very soft indeed'. If, on the other hand, an Irish person has just been conquered by the entire British Army and it starts lashing, that would be a very hard rain.

2) **Big rain:** A 'big rain' is one that starts in early January and lasts until the end of December – and sometimes even for months and years after that. Irish people will often look out their windows on 1 January and say: 'That looks like a big rain.' However, bookies stopped taking bets on whether a rain was going to be 'big' or not in 750 CE.

**3) Wet rain:** Contrary to popular belief and scientific fact, not all rain is wet. In Ireland you often get types that are dry, particularly if you're not standing outside in it. However, a 'wet rain' is one that will soak you right through, especially if you have to take your sheep for a long walk up a mountain or you decide to walk from Belfast to Cork in the middle of November just for fun.

**4) Rainy rain:** While this may sound like a childish description of rain, it accurately describes nearly every type Ireland has ever experienced, including the famous 'rainy rain' that fell on the county of Waterford from 1040 to 1140. That's not one hour, by the way, but one hundred years. No one really knows how Waterford got its name, but it could definitely be connected to the amount of water that fell in those years.

**5) Bloody rain:** Sometimes clouds pick up sand from the Sahara Desert, mix it with some moisture they happen to be carrying and then deposit it on Ireland, causing a fine red dust to cover everything, including Ford Cortinas, politicians and one's Sunday best. 'Bloody rain' doesn't, however, refer to this; it just refers to all rain, no matter what colour it is or how wet it is.

# 3
# SAVED BY A SLAVE

**Well, Holy God!**
As the fifth century dawned on the benighted island of Ireland, the 'new Irish' seemed fairly happy with their lot. They worked whenever they felt like it and had as little to do with godliness as possible, while their cleanliness was taken care of by the rather frequent occurrence of showers. They also liked to sing, dance and party like there was no tomorrow and no one true God. However, before long, they were to be proved wrong on both counts.

Even back then, there were concerned holy sorts who believed that it was no way to run a country and that it greatly reduced the chance of any Irish person making it as far as Heaven. These religious folk decided that what the Irish needed more than anything else was a very large dose of Christianity.

**Religious Order**
The problem was who to send to Ireland, which at that time was well known in religious circles as being a touch on the godless side, as well as rather cold, wet

and windy. Most missionaries had no problem going to nice, warm places like the south of France or Rio de Janeiro in order to do some conversions, but Hibernia (the wintry name had stuck despite the best attempts of the Pre-Christian Tourist Board of Ancient Ireland) was not top of their lists. Finally, after looking through thousands of CVs, the Vatican chose a Welsh slave as the perfect person to bring the word of God to the island. The man they selected was called Patrick, which was fortunate as almost all Irish people were also called Patrick or some variation thereof.

## Saint and Sinners

Saint Patrick, or just Pat as he was still known at the time, was dropped off in Ireland by the Vatican missionary ship in 432 CE, though it is not recorded if he got off without a fight. He started his holy work by doing the usual missionary stuff, such as standing on street corners and shouting stuff about God and how the Irish would all face eternal damnation if they didn't join the one true faith. However, most of them were too busy selling each other potatoes to notice him.

One man who happened to be passing and heard what he was saying, said: 'Eternal damnation couldn't be any worse than this, you daft Welshman!'

Patrick's faith wavered slightly at this point, but he persevered and decided to use that old fail-safe method, the miracle. He stood on top of a mountain and said quite loudly so he could be heard all over the island: 'In the name of God, I hereby banish all dinosaurs, koalas and Visigoths from the lands of the true and fiery Gael.'

However, a passer-by – it is not recorded but it may have been the same chap who made the eternal damnation comment earlier – pointed out: 'Sure, anyone can banish stuff we don't have, you dopey God-botherer!'

'Yes,' Patrick replied calmly, 'but this banishment also applies for the future too.'

'You mean that if koalas ever try to invade, we can just tell them that you said they weren't allowed to?' the passer-by said in a tone bordering on impertinent.

'Pretty much,' Patrick replied.

'You're mental,' the Irishman said and went off to buy some rain from a passing rain-seller.

### Three for One Special

Next, Patrick tried to teach them about the Holy Trinity. He believed that if they could grasp that concept, they would be well on the way to becoming Christians. He found another mountain and climbed to the top where he shouted: 'So it's like three things, but it's really only one!'

'What are you banging on about now?' asked a godless savage who looked suspiciously like the rather rude one from earlier.

'The Holy Trinity,' Patrick said. 'It's three in one.'

'You really are a nutter,' the man said.

'OK,' Patrick said. 'If I pick up three potatoes and hold them close together in my hand like this, how many have I got?'

**Saint Patrick teaches the Miracle of the Three Potatoes.**

'Three,' he said.

'OK, but what if I sort of mush them together like this?' Patrick asked, trying desperately not to lose his patience.

'Then you've got mashed potatoes,' the man said.

'Yes, but I have turned the three into one,' Patrick said.

'Eh, no, you haven't, Taffy,' he said, which was unchristian, mean and racist.

## The Patience of a Saint

On 17 March, a day still fondly remembered by Irish people everywhere, Patrick was wandering around looking for inspiration when he came across the potatoes he had previously been mashing together. They had somehow fallen into a dry spot and a liquid was oozing out which, though not pleasant to taste, made him feel very nice when he drank it.

Patrick then realised that they had fermented and distilled themselves into a form of alcohol – in other words, it was the miracle for which he had been searching. Delighted, he shouted: 'In the Bible, Jesus turned water into wine. I now have turned potatoes into booze. Behold the hand of God.'

That cheeky chap from before said he would give it a try. He drank several glasses and then threw his arms around Patrick and told him that he had misjudged him, that he loved him like a brother and that he was 'a goddamned saint'. Then all the Irish came over, drank lots of the potato alcohol and were the happiest they'd been in ... well, ever.

And when Patrick asked them if they were all Christians now, they said: 'Sure, why not? Three cheers for Paddy!'

## The Holy Land

And so Ireland became a Christian country and all the Gaels, who had always been a brave and fierce lot, went to Mass on Sunday mornings, belted each other with 'hurley' sticks in the afternoon and rejoiced that, thanks be to God, they had found yet another excellent use for the humble spud.

## A Successful Conversion Attempt

Back in the fifth century, it was well known that the Gaels, like most other primitive people, would basically worship anything, from the sun or the nearest river god to bats or even very large mushrooms.

From the diaries kept by Algernon T. Sweeney, a minor warlord living near Carlow, we can get a good impression of how this worshipping occurred:

> In order to settle a dispute between Malachus O'Malachi and Fringius MacAnaspie, I told them that my goat could sort it out. I said he was quite wise and holy, as goats go, and that he was 'inspired' by the Lord Buddha, a well-known Nepalese god. They didn't 'believe' at first, so I took a cudgel to them until they really 'believed'.
>
> Then I told them that if the goat, who I called King Poc, ran forwards, Malachus was in the right and if it ran backwards, Fringius was in the right. Poc, who was quite lazy and who I had tied firmly to a stake so he couldn't move, didn't go forwards or backwards. Malachus and Fringius asked me what this meant and

> *I told them that it was a miracle and that they each needed to give me 500 gold coins.*

These ancient belief systems suited the Irish until St Patrick arrived with his stories of Jesus Christ, the turning of water into wine and the holy potatoes. After that, Algernon quickly gave up being a Goat Buddhist and converted to Catholicism and, in line with his new religion, remained quite the sinner until he died of syphilis in 462.

**The movement of goats was often used to settle local 'religious' disputes.**

# Top Five

## Tastiest Dishes Invented by the Irish

As most people know, the Irish have been around for quite a long time. This is down to their determination to survive no matter what was thrown at them – and they've had their fair share of things thrown at them. Not least of these was an unforgiving terrain in which it was hard to grow anything. However, they overcame that and have given the world some very tasty dishes.

1) **Real Irish stew:** There are many different ways to make Irish stew, but the 'real' version is a complex mix of carefully chosen ingredients, subtle flavours and intricate seasoning. To make it, you collect everything edible you can find inside and outside the house and put it all into a huge saucepan filled with water. Then boil for six to eight weeks, hope for the best and serve.

2) **Crisp sandwich:** Considered a delicacy since medieval times, the crisp sandwich is a useful addition to the culinary canon as it can be eaten as breakfast, lunch or dinner, or all three if you're on holiday. Obviously, it is difficult to prepare unless you are a

trained chef, but the basic approach is to get two slices of white bread, butter them and put some crisps between them. You can then add various 'secret' ingredients, such as mayonnaise, tomato ketchup or whatever that relishy-looking stuff at the back of the fridge used to be.

**3) Sushi spuds:** While the Japanese like to take credit for creating raw fish, the Irish actually invented 'raw' cooking centuries before they did. They would basically dig a potato out of the earth, look at it briefly and then eat it. Centuries ago, these were known as 'organic' potatoes, as they were completely chemical free and generally covered in tasty black soil.

**4) Mushy veg:** As the real Irish stew above shows, one of the great secrets of Irish cooking is that if you leave something in boiling water for long enough, there's a good chance you will eventually be able to eat it. This is true for ferns, tree bark and many insects, though unfortunately not for bicycle tyres. It is very handy for vegetables, though, particularly for peas, which develop into a nice, watery pea-tasting mush after only a few hours of intense boiling.

**5) Cabbage surprise:** While the name of this dish might

suggest something surprising, it is, in fact, not surprising at all. It consists of cabbage and that's pretty much it. If you are having a dinner party, you can make it fancier by adding more cabbage, but as with so many other cabbage-based dishes, less is more.

# 4

# SO THAT'S WHY THEY CALL THEM THE DARK AGES

**Druids Versus Priests Versus the Irish**

The conversion of the Irish by St Patrick was generally seen as a good thing around the world, even though it led to a lot of conflict on the island. Even Pope Bruce VI, the only Australian pope in history, issued a press release: 'We are thrilled to welcome the fighting Irish into the Christian Church. We look forward to working with them for many years to come, but do hope they will stop killing each other (unless, of course, it's for sound religious reasons).'

As always, there were some people who were not too happy about the coming of Christianity. The main group opposed to it was the Affiliated Union of Druids, who looked after the spiritual welfare of the Celts and considered themselves the only mystic men Ireland needed.

St Patrick, however, had little time for them, even describing them in an article in *The Ancient Christian*

*Times* as 'low-rent Gandalfs ... though without his charm, style or magic'. This caused a lot of friction between priests and druids and you would often see them arguing in village squares. These arguments would frequently turn into full-scale fights, though God generally made sure his boys won out.

The druids even staged protests, strikes and go-slows, but eventually St Patrick just got tired of them and banished all druids from Ireland, with most of them leaving on the same ship as the snakes. (Note: some historians still contend that the druids just put on long black dresses and white collars and became priests.)

## The Particularly Dark Ages

No one was more pleased that they were all now Christian than the Irish themselves. Indeed, for the first few hours after the conversion went through, there was a lot of high-fiving, back-slapping and general merriment about the place. Far be it from historians to pass comment, but you could almost say the Irish were a little bit smug about their new-found holiness.

This smugness was short-lived, however. Almost immediately, all the holy men in the country started preaching. They told the people of Ireland, who had always loved a fight and a party (often at the same time) that those days were over. It wasn't long before the whole country was covered in priests and monks, as these were well-paid, high profile jobs with great prospects. While many were put off by not being allowed to hang out with women, some apparently even managed to find ways around that.

## A Wholly Holy Nation

The target for the Vatican and presumably for God himself was that Ireland should become the holiest nation on Earth. This meant that everyone in the country had to get up at 4 a.m. and pray while kneeling on sharp stones until 8 a.m. Then it was breakfast time, which consisted of cold porridge with small, grated pebbles mixed through it, all washed down with cups of cold, milky, sugarless tea, which was often made without using tea.

**Praying while kneeling on sharp stones
was good for the soul.**

Then, after breakfast at 8.02 a.m., everyone over
the age of four would go to work in the fields, where
they would collect sharp stones, or they would work
building churches and monasteries. By Vatican decree,
each town and village in Ireland was to have at least
four holy buildings, so there was plenty of God's work

to be done. The working day would finish at 11 p.m., which would be followed by six more hours of prayer, reflection and thanksgiving. By this time, most people would already be an hour late for morning prayers, which was punishable by having to pray an extra five hours every day.

As the Irish were now getting up when it was dark and going to bed when it was even darker, they called the following few hundred years the Dark Ages. It was a tough schedule, but everyone knew that if the Irish were going to make it to Heaven, they were going to have to suffer. A lot.

## When the Party's Over

It is not recorded if Irish people ever regretted taking the Christian path, as saying stuff like that out loud was punishable by whipping, which no one really liked. Historians can only speculate as to what would have happened if the Irish had told St Patrick where to get off and that they were happy without his fancy new religion. Certainly, Ireland would be a very different country today and might even have developed into a popular and much-visited snake sanctuary.

However, the power of the Irish to enjoy themselves no matter how bad things get should never be underestimated. While the immediate aftermath of conversion might have seen the people becoming all-religious, they were back having fun by the weekend.

The only difference now was that they had to do it behind the priests' backs.

The Irish are a resourceful bunch and it wasn't long before they were using every trick in the book to have fun. They still did the work and the praying, but they managed to squeeze in some good times between the cracks left by the priests. (Note: this might be where the 'Irish' word 'craic' comes from, but the Internet was down when we were working on this chapter, so we couldn't google it.)

While the priests and monks were off writing homilies, colouring in Bibles and chatting up women, the people of Ireland were singing, dancing and drinking to beat the band – unfortunately, a lot of bands tended to get beaten back then.

## Making Money by the Book

Even as far back as the Dark Ages, the Irish have always been an entrepreneurial bunch. One such businessperson was Veritas Sweeney of the Meath Sweeneys, who saw a huge opportunity when the Irish went all religious. Realising that the people would need lots of Bibles if they were to learn all the holy stuff that goes with modern religions, he set about writing out the Bible. This was many years before the invention of printing presses, photocopiers and 3D printers, so Veritas had to do everything himself. His first Bible, which took him twelve years to complete, sold for just £2.50 in old money.

Dismayed at the rather paltry return on investment, Veritas decided to set up a Bible-illustrating factory in his hometown. He hired hundreds of men, women, children and priests to sit for hour after hour knocking out illustrated versions of the Bible. He used a clever scheme whereby one group would knock out quick pencil outlines of Bible scenes. Each small section in these had a number which corresponded to a colour of paint, so all the next group of workers had to do was fill in each section and the Bible was ready.

Even though they were written in Latin, they sold really well, as even back then people loved cartoon books. It is believed that his Kells factory produced nearly four million books between 790 and 810, though only one remains in existence today. At the age of forty-two, Veritas himself retired on the profits to the Holy Land, though he was also spotted several times at the carnival in Rio.

# Top Five

## Most Accessible Religions the Irish Have Tried

The Irish have always been into their religion, but it wasn't just St Patrick's one that got them excited. Plenty of other belief systems were tried both before and after the arrival of Christianity.

1) **Sun worship:** Before the Irish discovered the real God, they were inclined to worship anything that took their fancy, like big rivers, trees that had fallen over and even particularly intelligent donkeys. However, their number one thing for worshipping was the sun. It was the perfect god, as it seemed very powerful, rarely ever appeared and lived in the sky. Irish people still worship the sun to this day, though mainly when they're abroad.

2) **New Ageism:** It is believed by some that well-known sage Gautama O'Buddha (or just 'Buddha') may have spent a summer in the west of Ireland as a student in the year 540 BCE, predating St Patrick's mission by about 1,000 years. However, no records whatsoever exist of his time there, and the only people who seem to believe it are some New Age

types, whom the local Garda sergeant says worship him by behaving like 'bloody students'.

3) **Merry Mysticism:** There is very little the Irish like doing more than getting closer to various gods, often when completely sober. However, one religious group discovered that they could also get next to him/her/them by getting very drunk indeed. Called the Merry Mystics, they drank all day and then just lay on the ground and stared at their god (or the sky) for ages. Some of the holier ones even spoke in tongues, chanted or just mumbled incoherently through their beards.

4) **Celticism:** From earliest times, Irish people have been a very spiritual and a very sporting people. They often worshipped their local sports team as much as God, whether that 'local' team was based in Ireland, Britain or somewhere further afield, such as Brazil. Celticism originally referred to supporters of Celtic Football Club in Glasgow, but now includes anyone who talks about sport as much as they talk about religion.

5) **Mammonism:** Until the late twentieth century Irish people had generally preferred worshipping gods that you couldn't see or touch. However, when the god Mammon landed in Dublin Airport in spring

1997 dressed up like a giant green tiger, quite a few people decided to worship him instead. This didn't work out too well, as it was eventually discovered that Mammon doesn't buy you happiness – or indeed eternal salvation.

# 5

# THE BLOODY VIKINGS ARE COMING!

**A Little Peace of Ireland**

The conversion of the entire population meant that Irish people could finally stop fighting and just be really nice and Christian to each other. It was a time of great harmony, peace and growth on the island, as everyone worked together to make Ireland into one of the world's greatest little countries. For example, if two warlords had a disagreement over who owned a particular tree, sheep or plot of land, they would just say to each other: 'Hey, we're all Christians now, so no fighting! Let's cut it in two and take half each. Then, if you're up for it, maybe we could say a prayer or two together.'

**And the Future was Looking so Bright**

The good times also saw religion and culture flourish in Ireland, as people devoted less time to scrapping and more time to reading the Bible, praising God and punishing themselves for being sinners. When all the praying was done, the Irish would relax by going to a 'public house', which was very like a church. The main difference was that in these 'pubs' they could talk about all the nice religious stuff they had done during the day while sipping quietly on some mead or some of the 'holy water' St Patrick had invented. This was a wonderful time to be Irish and everybody was delighted to put the years of war behind them forever and ever.

Unfortunately, the peace and harmony of the island was about to be shattered and not just for a few decades, but for hundreds of years to come.

## Of all the Countries in all the World …

On a quiet summer's day in 795 CE, most of the Irish were on the beach sheltering from the wind when one sharp-eyed young man spotted a ship heading straight for the shore.

'Look, a ship heading straight for the shore,' he said, as he was a very straight-talking sort of chap. Another man stood beside him and agreed. 'It could be our latest shipment of Bibles arriving from Rome,' he said. 'Or it could be those aubergines we ordered from India.'

'Whoever they are, they are making a lot of noise and they're wearing extremely silly hats,' a woman said. 'Let's hope it's not a stag party!'

Then a wise man, who was trying to figure out why he was on the beach in the first place as he hated sand getting in his sandwiches, said: 'I wouldn't worry too much. As long as it's not a ship full of marauding Vikings, we should be just fine.' And he wandered off to advise some local men that if you're building a monastery out of sand, you should build it nearer the shore, so you could use 'the wet sand'.

Unfortunately, the wise man was perhaps not quite as wise as he thought he was, and it did turn out to be a ship full of marauding Vikings. Interestingly, the famous Sand Monastery of Ballyratchet is also no longer standing.

## Vicious, Violent and Viking

The Irish were no match for the Vikings, who were tall, blond, blue-eyed, handsome and extremely vicious. At first, the Irish offered to turn the other cheek, as they had been instructed to do by the Bible. Unfortunately, turning your other cheek to a Viking generally meant you had your head cut off twice, which was twice as painful and doubly effective.

The Vikings were also masters at pillaging and plundering. In fact, lexicographers of the time had to invent both those words just to describe the raiding, looting, robbing, marauding, burning, slaughtering, hacking, thieving and butchering which the Vikings just loved to do.

Eventually, the Irish did put up something of a fight, though this often took the form of hiding their villages behind large forests and directing the Vikings towards some of the larger monasteries instead.

## Long Day's Journey into Nightcaps

After a long day pillaging and plundering – everyone knows how tiring that can be – the Vikings went to a local pub for a pint, a ham-and-cheese toastie and a sing-song. It was on these long nights that the Vikings and the Irish got to know each other.

'Ah, you're all right, Paddy,' a Viking would say.

'You're not so bad yourself, Bjorn, Erik or whatever your name is,' the Irishman would reply. 'And I tell you what: if you don't batter me tomorrow, you can marry my Rosaleen *and* I'll tell you where the monks stash all their fancy golden chalices.'

'Is that Rosaleen over there?' the Viking would ask. 'Listen, Mick, I don't want to be rude, but you don't have any other daughters, do you?'

This friendly banter eventually led to various alliances being formed between the native Irish and the Vikings. The canny Irish also decided to learn stuff from the Vikings, who were good at sailing, trading and building towns. In return, the Irish taught them how to pray, make mashed potatoes and where to find the best pint.

## Friends and Enemies

However, the longer the Vikings stayed in Ireland, the lazier they became. They also began to act as if they owned the place, which was beginning to get on the nerves of the natives. Eventually, it just got too much for the Irish and they decided they would politely ask the Vikings to leave. When that didn't work, they declared centuries of war on all tall, blond foreign types.

After an awful lot of fighting and with no victor emerging, the two sides then decided to have a winner-takes-all battle. This was scheduled to take place in Clontarf in north Dublin in 1014.

Fortunately, the Irish had on their side the bravest man who ever lived, Brian Boru, the undisputed High King of Ireland and slaughterer of millions of Vikings. The Vikings, on the other hand, only had Sitric Silkenhead, Rupert Rufflefeathers and Timothy Tigglebottom on their side. With names like that, there was only going to be one winner, even if Brian Boru's forces were greatly outnumbered.

Unfortunately, while the Irish were celebrating their victory with a traditional knees-up in the Gravedigger's Pub in Glasnevin, which was a mere bus ride away from Clontarf, a Viking dressed as a native snuck in and assassinated Brian Boru. It wasn't the best end to what had been a great day for the Irish.

**The original Millennium Spire in 988.**

## A Capital Intervention

In the year 988, a relatively poor chieftain called Ignatius 'Iggy' Sweeney of the Fairview Sweeneys happened to be out walking his Irish wolfhounds near the Black Pool of Leinster when he came across a bunch of Vikings. They were getting into their dinghy so they could reach their ship anchored in the bay.

'Story, lads?' Iggy said, using the standard Dublin greeting of the time.

'God dag,' one of the taller, blonder and beardier Vikings said, which Ignatius thought was a bit rude and possibly blasphemous. 'All the land has been pillaged and plundered and there is nothing left for us here, so we are going to cross the ocean to the US of A.'

'Really?' asked Iggy. And then, like a lot of people from that part of Ireland, he had a crafty idea. 'If youse give me your boat, right, you can have my land. It stretches from here to those mountains and has a bunch of rivers, two canals and a millennium spire.'

The Vikings were delighted with this offer, so Iggy jumped into the dinghy and headed off.

'What's it called?' the Vikings shouted after him.

'I call it a kip, but you can call it Black Pool,' he shouted back. 'And if you see a rather large, bossy-looking woman, will you tell her I always loved her ... and probably always will, and that I may write?'

And so the capital of Ireland, Blackpool, was founded. The name was later changed to the Irish version Dublin, as English people kept going there on holiday by mistake.

# Top Five

## Useful Inventions You Didn't Know Were Irish

The Irish have always been an enterprising and inventive lot and have given the world many wonderful things, such as the submarine, colour photography and shorthand. They also came up with lots of clever ideas that were made into practical inventions by others much later on.

**1) The aeroplane:** Long before Leonardo da Vinci invented the helicopter or the Wright brothers flew their first plane, the Irish had been experimenting with human flight, though often with mixed and sometimes fatal results. They got their original inspiration for flight from winged animals known as 'birds'. Line drawings of men with wings found in caves suggest that 'early' Irish people wanted to fly, though they may just not have been very good at drawing birds.

**2) The smoothie:** Although it was originally called a 'roughie', the Irish invented this popular drink in the eleventh century as a way of using up some of the less popular vegetables. They would painstakingly cut them up into really small pieces and then 'drink' the mixture. It was considered a healthy option and saved time on boiling.

**3) Velcro:** While they may not have actually invented it, the Irish saw the need for a substance like Velcro many years before it was developed. For centuries before Christianity, men and women wandered around with their jackets hanging open and their trousers falling down. Obviously, this situation couldn't continue once religion entered the equation, so the Irish cleverly came up with various versions of Velcro, including double-sided sticky tape, honey spread on a piece of cloth and the zip.

**4) The umbrella:** There have been many different incarnations of the umbrella throughout history, but the one used by early settlers in Ireland may have been the first. They came up with the idea of a reversible umbrella, which actually collected rainwater as opposed to letting it go to waste. They walked around with these on their heads and if they got thirsty they would just scoop out a cup of lovely, fresh water.

**5) iGlasses:** As hard as it may be to believe now, the Irish invented a high-tech version of Google Glasses in the nineteenth century. They basically consisted of a frame with two pieces of glass and enabled the wearer to see the whole world through them – or at least whatever part of the whole world they happened to be in at the time. As well as being called iGlasses, they are sometimes referred to as eyeglasses, spectacles or just glasses.

# 6
# DANGER HERE!

**All the best families fought their way through the Dark Ages.**

**Feuding Families Fighting Fit**

Brian Boru was one of the greatest High Kings of all time and would easily have made a top ten list if they had taken the time to do such things back then. He had united the entire country through respect, fear and a fair amount of bloodshed. His death in Clontarf in 1014 was not good news for anyone, least of all Brian himself.

The vacuum left afterwards was filled by lots of not-so-high kings trying to claim Ireland for themselves, as family waged war on family. For example, the O'Connors decided to invade the land of the O'Rourkes while they were busy fighting the O'Neills. As a result, the O'Donnells stepped in and started picking on the Murphys, which really pissed off the O'Rahillys. And, obviously when you piss off the O'Rahillys, you upset the MacMahons, the McCarthys, the O'Sullivans and the Mancinis. Although the Mancinis should probably have minded their own business, because they were 'only a bunch of pizza-selling blow-ins' as that well-known racist and troublemaker Dermot Mac Murrough once called them. If Dermot hadn't been King of Leinster and a dab hand at getting out of tight spots, he could have got himself into a lot of hot water over that comment.

**A Little Adultery Can Go a Long Way**

As well as being a racist and a troublemaker, the 'bould' Dermot Mac Murrough was also a first-class adulterer at a time when adultery was neither popular nor profitable, particularly if you got caught. It was Dermot's love of the ladies that changed the course of Irish history more than any other single event, including the coming of Christianity, the discovery of the pint and Riverdance being the interval act at the 1994 Eurovision Song Contest. Dermot's seduction – though some historians prefer to call it an abduction – of the wife of his rival, Tiernan O'Rourke of Breifne, did not go down well with anybody, least of all with Tiernan himself. Unfortunately, it is not recorded what his wife thought about it, as historians at the time rarely sought women's opinions on such matters.

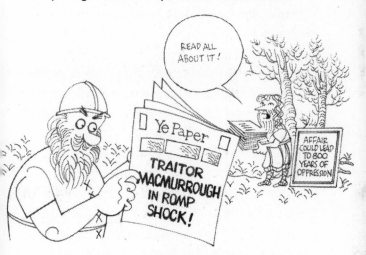

**Dermot Mac Murrough's affair even made the tabloids.**

One very drunken night, Tiernan and his best mate Rory O'Connor, who was the Highest King of All-Ireland at the time, got together and drove Dermot out of Ireland. They didn't literally 'drive him out' as they were far too drunk; they just sort of threatened to beat him up if he didn't leave before breakfast the following morning.

It wasn't to be the last time that women and alcohol were to prove a heady mix for Ireland's destiny. (This isn't really a historic fact, but is included here because it sounds sort of dramatic and portentous.)

## The Luck of the Irish

In a similar situation, it has to be said that very few Irishmen would have done what Dermot did next: begged for help from the king of England. Interestingly, neither nation had really taken much notice of the other until that fateful day in 1166 when Dermot pitched up outside Buckingham Palace (or wherever Henry II lived), telling tall tales about loose women tempting him and drunken men bullying him.

Although Henry II was generally anti-bullying, he told Dermot he couldn't help him out as he was too busy bullying his own people. He did say that if Dermot could convince his Norman vassals to help him, then he could use them, as long as he gave them lots of stout, women and land in return.

However, Henry also said Dermot would need the approval of a pope. Fortunately for them – and unfortunately for Ireland – the pope at the time was a young Cockney lad called 'Arry, the first, last and probably only English pope ever (apart, of course, from Pope Adrian IV, who died in 1159). He said Henry could invade wherever he wanted as far as he was concerned – which, in the case of Ireland, clearly wasn't very far at all.

'That's the luck of the Irish for you,' Henry said sarcastically about this turn of events.

## The Name's Bow, Strongbow!

The Normans arrived in Ireland in 1169, led by the rather girlishly named Richard de Clare, Second Earl of Pembroke. Immediately, the Irish laughed at him, figuring they could easily defeat someone with such a fancy name. He promptly changed his name to Strongbow, got a tattoo of a very big arrow on his forearm and subjugated the entire country in about two hours. The Irish learned a valuable lesson that morning: never slag a Norman to his face; it is much safer to do it behind his back.

After he had won every battle going, Strongbow realised that he quite liked the Irish sense of humour – as long as he wasn't the butt of their jokes. He decided to settle down in Dublin, marry a nice local girl and get a safe 'office' job. The girl he married was Aoife, daughter of Dermot Mac Murrough, so Strongbow knew he had to keep an eye on her as, if her morals were anything like her father's, she was going to be a handful.

**The fighting in Ireland went on and on ... and on.**

### Now It's the Bloody English

With Strongbow and his Norman buddies making themselves at home, Henry began to worry that he was missing out on some great conquest action. To remedy this, he decided he would head over to Ireland himself and let them all know who the real boss was. This made Henry the first English king ever to set foot on Irish soil and led to more than 800 years of very close associations between the two countries.

Interestingly, many Irish chieftains and warlords actually welcomed Henry with open arms and had no problem submitting to his will. Clearly, they had realised their mistake with Strongbow and figured that pretending to like a violent, foreign invader was a better strategy.

## You'll Never Fool the English

Back in the fourteenth century, an Irish chieftain living in the west of Ireland called Aloysius Sweeney of the Clifden Sweeneys was fairly happy with his life. He was king of all his land, which stretched from the mountain to the tree to the well and back to his castle. He had a large family, a bunch of subjects who worked his land and three pet bunnies called Cuddles, Puddles and Muddles. (Note: the rabbits are not historically relevant to this incident, but are included to lend colour.)

One day, however, the English army arrived, conquered everything in sight and made Aloysius swear allegiance to their king. Aloysius decided that the safest thing to do was to go along with whatever these men wanted, as fighting them seemed like a losing battle, particularly as they were heavily armed and ruthless in a posh, evil sort of way.

This arrangement suited all concerned and life went on much as before. However, as things were getting busy with the harvest approaching, Aloysius politely asked the soldiers to help out. Their commander, Baron Cecil Beatington Smythe III, agreed as long as he could marry Pádraiga, Aloysius's niece. Eventually, Aloysius even persuaded his new nephew-in-law that he should also help out around the place. Thanks to all the new workers, Aloysius managed to become richer than ever before. He even persuaded the soldiers to help him to defeat his neighbours and deadliest rivals, the MacBrides and the Kavanaghs.

As Aloysius wrote in his memoir, *How To Make Fools of Invaders Without Their Knowing*: 'The English? Best thing ever happened to me.' It wasn't a view shared by many outside his realm, but then the book was only on sale in his kingdom, where it remained at the top of the best-seller list for more than forty years.

# Top Five

## Useful Things the Irish Robbed from the English

It is a well-known historical fact that the English are the poshest people on the planet and have super manners. Even when they colonise you, they are generally quite polite about it. However, it is a credit to the Irish that they learned to live with all of that. Indeed, the Irish actually profited from the English conquest by 'borrowing' many of their greatest assets and using them for themselves.

1) **The English language:** Speaking Irish or Gaelic was all very well if you had other people you could speak it to. Unfortunately, that ruled out most of the planet, so the Irish decided to learn English. This came in very handy when the Irish themselves tried to conquer the world through emigration.

2) **Manners:** By all accounts, they don't cost a lot, and as the English were really good at them, the Irish watched and learned. When they got good at manners, they even realised that if you were polite to the English and said things like, 'Gosh, turn around and look over there please!' you could hit them over the head much more easily.

3) **Sports:** Irish sport generally consisted of throwing potatoes at people on the opposite team or running around hitting each other over the head with big sticks. So when they saw gentlemanly English sports like soccer and cricket, they eventually decided to adopt them and turn them into proper

manly contact sports, such as Gaelic football and hurling (see p. 121).

4) **Shopping:** Before the English came along, the Irish used to have different shops for every single item on their lists, meaning a shopping trip could take up to twelve days to complete, as you would have to go to the potato market, the turnip shop, the cabbage emporium and many, many others. The English 'supermarket' changed all that and left the Irish more time to practise their English, their manners and their revenge.

5) **Television:** In the bad old days, the Irish used to sit around telling stories, drinking whiskey and singing sad songs about the fact that television was yet to be invented. The English changed all that and showed the Irish that there was more to life and that it could all fit inside a small box.

# 7
# KING TO QUEEN
# TO CHECKMATE

**An English Solution to an Irish Problem**
And so began eight centuries of fun, games and oppression. From the twelfth century on, the English
did everything in their power to make the Irish more
'English', including teaching them tiddlywinks, making
them eat Yorkshire pudding and, when all else failed,
taking their lives. The Irish are a famously stubborn
lot, however, and very little worked. Often, the Irish
would just turn around to their conquerors and say:
'Yip, that's grand, we're all English now, so you fellas
can head off home and we'll look after things here for
you.'

The English usually replied: 'How jolly decent of
you! Back home, they told us you were savages, but
you chaps are actually quite good sports!'

And the Irish would reply: 'Not a bother, me lord
sir! See youse later.'

Then, as soon as the English were gone, they would
just carry on being all Irish, having fun and staying up

late telling stories about how they managed to dupe the English.

However, the English soon realised that their policy of absenteeism was becoming a joke. They knew that the best way to defeat the cunning Irish was to suppress the entire country, which would have cost a fortune ... or they could just build a big wall around the greater Dublin area and put signs on it saying, 'Beyond this wall is Britain. No Irish, no savages, no dogs!' They decided on the less painful latter option and called the walled area The Pale. These days The Pale is protected by the fast and dangerous M50 ring road instead of a big wall, though most people who live outside it have little or no desire to enter.

## More Irish than the Irish Themselves

Ironically, the Norman and English policy of trying to make the Irish less Irish backfired, and by the fifteenth and sixteenth centuries a lot of the former oppressors had become more Irish than the Irish themselves. First among these were the Fitzgeralds, the Earls of Kildare, who looked Irish, ate chips a lot and wore Celtic football shirts. They were descended from a man called Norman Fitzgerald, who, as his name suggests, was more Norman than most Normans. He had been a big pal of Strongbow's back in the day, but his descendants were now plotting a way to be independent from the English crown.

That particular crown was being worn by Henry VIII at the time and the Fitzgeralds decided it would be best to butter him up and pretend they were ruling Ireland in his name. The other option would have been a massive war, which would have definitely got in the way of traditional leisure pursuits such as coursing, cursing and just hanging out. This arrangement also suited Henry VIII, as he had a lot of domestic issues to deal with. Well, six to be exact.

## Horrid Henry Divorces the Church

Henry's home life also rather famously caused a row with the Church, which wasn't keen on people divorcing their wives, let alone beheading them. This meant that a split with Rome was inevitable. Naturally,

Henry decided to become head of his very own Church and dissolved all the monasteries in England and Ireland. This led Garrett Óg Fitzgerald to quip: 'As long as "Pope Henry the Wife-Murderer" doesn't dissolve the pubs, we shouldn't have a problem.'

Unfortunately, someone told Henry about this particular gag, which led him to crush the Fitzgeralds and force his rule on all Irish clans. He did this using the 'Surrender and Regrant' policy, which meant that if you surrendered to him, he wouldn't kill you and you could keep your land, which was doubly nice of him. The Irish chieftains agreed, but only because it didn't really affect them either way.

## The Virgin Queen: A Mostly Lovely Girl

When Elizabeth I ascended to the English throne in 1558, she took a more lenient attitude towards Ireland, because 'the trendy young queen is desperate to find a husband, get married and settle down'. (Note: this rather sexist comment appeared in an editorial in the December 1558 edition of *Hello!* magazine and is not a historical fact.) She even let the people of Ireland carry on being Catholic, speak their own language and live, which was dead nice of her.

In return, all she wanted from the various chieftains who had divided the country up between them was 'unconditional loyalty', the swearing of an odd oath and bucket-loads of cash. This suited everyone – until some of the Irish fellas got greedy and started scrapping with their neighbours over bits of land. This led to Elizabeth showing her not so lovely side and coming down quite hard on the Irish.

Eventually, in 1607, four years after Elizabeth's death, a bunch of Irish earls decided enough was enough. They were going to go to Europe and bring back a fierce army that would defeat the English and end the conquest of Ireland forever and ever. Unfortunately, as the weather and the food were so lovely on the continent, they stayed there and never came back. This was known as The Cowardly Flight of the Earls, though the earls later shortened it to the much more catchy 'Flight of the Earls'.

**Queen Elizabeth was nice to the Irish – at first.**

## If You Can't Beat Them, Make Them Join You

Tired of fighting, the English then decided the best way to 'civilise' the Irish was to send some nice English, Scottish and Welsh people to live on their lands, so the Irish could see just how brilliant being British was. These 'Plantations' might have worked too, except that a lot of the planters weren't very brilliant – or very nice. They hadn't signed up for it because they loved the Irish and wanted to make them better people; they came because they were given free land with free peasants (or 'slaves') to work on it. It was lovely in theory, but probably not a recipe for success on the ground.

## Please Tell Me That's Not Cromwell

Until the seventeenth century war in Ireland had been mainly about unimportant things such as land, money and power, but after the Reformation and Counter-Reformation, it became more about good, old-fashioned religion. How God felt about this change was anyone's guess.

In 1649, when the latest war in England ended and Charles I lost his head and couldn't find it anywhere, the English sent over a lovely chap by the name of Oliver Cromwell. He was only in Ireland for nine months, but managed to get in more violence than many other English people had done in decades.

His theory of how to win a war – and it has yet to

be proved wrong – was to kill everybody. He and his army – they were originally going to call it the New 'Slaughter Everybody' Army but eventually decided on the much catchier New Model Army – basically attacked anyone they met who wasn't one of their soldiers.

Many English people look on Cromwell as a great hero and a military genius; Irish people, on the other hand, lean more towards the genocidal nutcase description. However he was viewed, he certainly made his mark on Ireland. The Act of Settlement of 1652 basically meant that if you were Irish, Catholic or just in the way, you could be slaughtered and have your land confiscated. The only other option was ... actually, in typical Cromwellian fashion, there wasn't any other option.

## Oliver's Army

The Irish are a generous people and are never keen to criticise anybody, even if that person's sole aim is to wipe them off the face of the planet. They were even quite nice about Oliver Cromwell. The following is a selection of quotes from various members of the Sweeney clan who knew and loved the real Oliver Cromwell:

- Ah, sure, he wasn't the worst by any means. Yes, he slaughtered all of us, including me, my wife and the kids, but who wouldn't have done the same in his situation? Just doing his job.

- Religious type, as far as I remember. Big into all the God stuff. And golf. Yeah, God, golf and killing Irish people: those were his things!

- Complete loony!

- Good-looking chap and could really hold a tune. Also a sharp dresser. But apart from that, a bit of a bastard.

- Complete bitch and I really doubt he was a virgin! Or is that Queen Elizabeth I'm thinking of? Now she was a piece of work, not that I ever met her. Cute nose, though! Or was that Cleopatra?

- Total psycho.

- A gentleman through and through. You really couldn't have met a nicer chap. And a professional, a consummate professional. If you wanted Irish Catholics taken care of, he was your only man.

# Top Five

## Moving Statutes That Made The Natives Restless

The 1366 Statutes of Kilkenny comprised thirty-five acts and were designed to preserve the joys of Norman rule in

Ireland by stopping the natives from acting overly Irish. A poll in the 1367 summer edition of *Medieval Cosmo* found that these were the top five most popular statutes of the time.

1) **Statute 7:** 'All English settlers must wear English clothes, such as those worn by traditional Morris dancers or in period dramas made by the BBC (as and when it is eventually established).'

2) **Statute 14:** 'No English people are allowed to marry Irish people. Or kiss them. Actually, even holding hands is out of the question ... except maybe at summer music festivals and if there is drink taken.'

3) **Statute 15:** 'The adoption of Irish children by Englishers is strictly forbidden for fear that the little "Gaelic thugs" might contaminate English homes with their horrid Irishness.'

4) **Statute 22:** 'English people must only speak English. They must never use the natives' rather ugly language. In fact, they should never speak to the natives unless they are ordering them to fetch stuff or clean their feet.'

5) **Statute 35:** 'The only sports to be played must be English ones. These include cricket, rugger, polo (of the horsey variety) and peasant-hunting (on

foot or horseback). The following Irish sports are outlawed and if anyone is seen playing them, they are to be put to death on the spot (with a possible trial at a later date): potato-throwing, goat-chasing and rock-bouncing.'

# 8

# A BLIGHT ON THE LANDSCAPE

Religion made it hard to know
whose side you were on.

## War But Not Much Peace

Oliver Cromwell's policy of dispatching 'anyone who looks vaguely Irish' was an effective and straightforward solution to the problem of the Irish. However, it was time-consuming and expensive, so the English decided to keep taking Irish land and pushing the peasants further west across the country (and towards America). Things were also getting more and more complicated as you now had Irish Protestants, English Catholics, royalist Catholics, rebel Protestants, Catholic Protestants and even Protestant Protestants. It was becoming increasingly difficult for people to know whose side they were supposed to be on.

The Williamite Wars went some way to sorting this mess out, with William of Orange's smashing defeat of James II's forces at the Battle of the Boyne finally letting Catholics know their place, which apparently was just below that of Protestants.

Although defeated in battle, it was also important to make sure the Catholics stayed crushed. This led to the introduction of the Penal Laws, which were like the Statutes of Kilkenny only more so. They included bans on Catholics enjoying nice weather, making fun of posh people and shooting English settlers with catapults.

## Unholy Union

Catholics were willing to accept these new, improved restrictions on their human rights for two reasons: one, they had no choice, and two, they just ignored them anyway. As a result, everyone got on relatively well together for the next century or so. As Anglo-Irish satirist Jonathan Swift might have put it in his early work, *An Immodest Proposal*: 'If the peasants aren't revolting, there's no point massacring them.'

As time passed and everyone seemed vaguely content not to scrap, the Irish parliament in Dublin began relaxing the restrictions. As long as there was loyalty to the crown and a few quid being sent to England, Westminster was happy to allow Ireland more autonomy.

Indeed, were it not for some meddling Protestant types, Ireland would probably still be a loyal colony to this day. However, towards the end of the eighteenth century, men such as Wolfe Tone had to go and stick their noses in, leaving the English no choice but to get tough again.

This rebellious activity eventually led to the Act of Union of 1800, which allowed Catholic emancipation but which also created the United Kingdom of Great Britain and Ireland. However, politics, war and acts of union were all about to become minor issues, as a well-known tuber was about to raise its potato-head above the parapet.

**Potatoes were extremely popular in the
nineteenth century.**

## A Feast of Spuds

Ireland had been a rural society since the first settlers
had managed to grow rocks in the harsh, unforgiving
soil. When it was discovered that they were difficult
to eat and almost impossible to digest, the Irish began
planting the next best thing: potatoes. Unlike rocks,
potatoes became even more edible when you boiled
them for a few hours.

There is a lot of debate about when the potato was introduced to Ireland. Some historians argue that Ireland was covered in potatoes from just after the Big Bang. Others say it was brought here and cultivated about sixty-five million years ago by a dinosaur called the Tuberosaurus. This is unlikely because dinosaurs weren't known for being great farmers. Religious historians, on the other hand, argue that God invented the potato and snuck one into St Patrick's man bag (or 'holy satchel') when he travelled here as a missionary. And, of course, Sir Walter Raleigh said he captured one in South America and brought it back alive to Europe. However, this is unlikely, as the Irish would never have fallen in love with a vegetable discovered by an Englishman.

Whichever theory is correct – and it's important to consider all theories just in case – one thing is true: the Irish love their spuds. Not only do they eat them, but they also used to use them to make clothes, construct cathedrals and throw at annoying foreigners.

## The Really Super Great Famine

Apart from conquest by the English, Roy Keane not playing in the 2002 World Cup and Dustin the Turkey not winning the 2008 Eurovision Song Contest, the worst crisis ever endured by the Irish people was the Really Great Potato Famine of 1845–48. It was particularly harsh as a rather cruel proviso in the Penal Laws meant that all Irish citizens had to live on potatoes, near potatoes or, if they were very poor, under potatoes.

Then evil English scientists working in the Royal Laboratory for Inventing Vegetable Diseases in Leighton Buzzard came up with a disease called blight, which was ideal for destroying potatoes. Almost overnight, there was nothing left for Irish people to eat – or turn into alcohol.

While most ordinary people struggled to survive this latest 'dirty trick' by the English, a group of Irish 'politicians' decided to hold an emergency meeting in Tara to discuss the crisis. Like politicians to this day, they desperately sought an Irish solution to this Irish problem, though they were roundly ignored by the general populace. For example, one of them stood up and said: 'The potato crop has failed. Let's all die.' This was met with murmurings of disapproval by the others, as it was agreed that starving to death was not an ideal solution.

Then, just as they were about to break for a pint and a bag of chips, another bright spark piped up and said: 'Wait a second: what about fish?' There was silence for a few minutes as the politicians tried to figure out if they should go for a pint first and discuss the fish idea later. Before they could, he added: 'Let's all grow gills, become fish and swim underwater to another land where they also have lots of potatoes.'

'No, you fool, we can't swim like fish,' another said. 'What we need to do is build vessels that will travel underwater like fish and take us to another land where they have lots of spuds.'

'Wow, that's a brilliant idea,' a third said. 'We could call them "sub marines".'

'Wait, I have another idea,' the second politician said. 'Why don't we build a ship that can go on top of the water and then sail to the other land with lots of potatoes?'

'Yes,' said the first man again, 'and we can call them "over-water sub-marines".'

These were later known as 'coffin ships', while the people at similar meetings are still known as politicians and are still coming up with ways to make life harder for ordinary people.

**Holyhead: the Welsh for Hollywood.**

## Last Ship to 'Hollywood'

The Great Famine was obviously not that 'great' if you were poor, Irish and big into potatoes. While many people perished in Ireland, many more escaped on various ships and then died on them. If you survived, a new life awaited you in England, America or Australia, where you could become a policeman, a nurse or a stereotype.

One Irishman who tried to help people escape was Wolfgang Amadeus FitzSweeney, one of the Celtic-Viking-Norman-English FitzSweeneys. He was one of the few 'Irish' people of the time to own his own company, which was called Promised Land Ltd. It was basically a fishing boat, which he operated out of Dun Laoghaire in South County Dublin. For a small fee, he would take people on his boat and bring them all the way to America. He also offered leisure activities on board, such as fishing. Actually, there was only fishing and Wolfgang kept all the fish.

When they arrived in the 'Promised Land', Wolfgang would point to the big sign saying 'Holyhead' and tell his passengers: 'Not only have I taken you all the way to America, but as a special favour I took you all the way around to Hollywood, which will soon be the hippest place on Earth.'

Very few Irish people could read, but those that could pointed out that the sign said 'Holyhead', not 'Hollywood'. To which Wolfgang would reply: 'Holyhead is American for Hollywood, you silly, hungry eejit.'

Wolfgang never felt bad about this minor deception because he reckoned he had still saved their lives, as very few would have survived the trip to the real Hollywood. To this day, there is believed to be a community of Irish people living in Holyhead in west Wales who think they are in America.

# Top Five

## Irish Emigrants Who Conquered the World

During the Great Famine, the Irish began to spread their wings and ended up making names for themselves in nearly every other country going. Great men like Bernardo O'Higgins, Clark Kent and Mahatma Gandhi all had Irish roots (except for Gandhi). However, there were a few other members of the diaspora who the Irish aren't so proud to celebrate and who don't even exist on the Internet.

1) **Mick 'Freedom' O'Murphy (1830–1874):** According to his autobiography, *Freedom Fighter*, the Monaghan-born O'Murphy liberated the island nation of Santa Corona in 1856, though he neglects to say who he liberated it from or even where it was. Nowadays, it's still quite hard to find on a

map, but back then Santa Corona was, according to O'Murphy himself, 'a huge country with a huger population. Honest!'

2) **Colman the Cowpoke (1858–1871):** Like Billy the Kid, Colman the Cowpoke didn't have a very tough-sounding nickname. Despite this, he did his best to become one of the most feared outlaws in the Wild West. Unfortunately, his best wasn't nearly good enough and he was shot dead in his first fight by Bonnie Bergin, another Irish outlaw and, coincidentally, his big sister.

3) **Teddy Boy Larraghy (1876–1905):** While he made quite a name for himself in Australia, he is not talked about much in his hometown. In fact, the people of Farrentooley deny he even came from there. Alleged to have murdered 3,000 people 'for fun', he was sentenced to death in 1905 and was hanged, drawn, hanged again, shot, quartered, hanged four times (because he was in quarters), drowned, burned and then buried alive.

4) **Timmy 'Two Ears' Tuohy (1888–1941):** Irish-Americans were famous for being either law-breakers or law-enforcers, but Timmy was both. He grew up in Boston where he became a beat cop; however, every Friday, he would make the long

drive to Chicago and become a gangster for the weekend. He was arrested in 1941 and was told he could fight in the army for six months or serve one year in prison. He chose the army and died in Pearl Harbor two days later when he was hit by a drunk Kamikaze pilot.

5) **Nuala 'Wrong Hands' O'Hurley (1942–):** Born in London's East End to Irish parents, Nuala became the most fearsome gangster in the city in the 1960s and was an ex-girlfriend of both Kray brothers. The relationships didn't last as they were 'petrified' of her. She had a taste for whiskey, cocaine and assault weapons, which could be a lethal combination in the wrong hands (hence her nickname). Imprisoned in 1975, she was released in 2009 and now runs an organised crime family in Sicily and New Jersey.

# 9

# FIGHTING WARS AND FIGHTING WORDS

## Independent States of Mind

Presumably the English would have been happy enough for the Irish to die from lack of potatoes as it would have saved money on expensive items such as soldiers, bullets and pikes. (Note: pikes were a type of long, thrusting spear, but for some bizarre reason the English also used the big, ugly freshwater fish of the same name to attack Irish peasants.)

However, the brave Irish were never going to be killed lying down. At the very least, they were going to stand up, fight, get killed and then lie down. As early as the late eighteenth century, men such as Wolfe Tone were prepared to die for Irish freedom. His United Irishmen would have had a good chance of getting somewhere if their French allies had managed to land at Bantry Bay in time for the revolution. Unfortunately, it was drizzling 'rather 'eavily' when they arrived, so instead of going ashore, the French headed back to Le Havre where they had a lovely lunch of frogs' legs, snails and other stereotypical French food. Meanwhile, the Irish got decimated (and very wet).

Various other battles against British forces took place along the east coast in Wexford and Wicklow and in the north, often with Catholics and Protestants happily fighting alongside each other for Irish independence. Well, happily until they all lost.

## Talking 'Bout a Revolution

The Act of Union meant the Irish had no political autonomy, and many now felt the only way to get independence was via Westminster. It is also possible that young Robert Emmet's valiant yet ultimately doomed actions (see p. 101) encouraged others in the nineteenth century to cut back on the violence and concentrate more on the talking, which was generally considered to be a lot less harmful to one's health.

One such man was Daniel O'Connell. Described in *The Munsterman* in July 1829 as 'Ireland's answer to Lincoln, Gandhi and Mandela', he founded the Catholic Association, which was a bit like the YMCA, except that it wasn't restricted to young men. It should also be pointed out that 1970s' disco group Village People also never wrote a song about O'Connell's Catholic Association. That we know of.

O'Connell's power lay in his ability as a fine lawyer, brilliant orator and non-stop talker. Lines such as 'Liberty is not worth the shedding of a single drop of blood', 'Will you please stop oppressing us?' and 'Has anyone seen my pet turtle?' really endeared him to his fellow countrymen. He even managed to rally enough Catholics behind him to win a seat in Westminster in 1828. Once in London, he swore he couldn't remember the wording of the vow that he was supposed to take before entering parliament. This pretence lasted for nineteen days, until the English gave up, granted Ireland Catholic emancipation and went home exhausted.

That wasn't the end of O'Connell, though: the

man they called 'The Liberator' went on a long tour of Ireland, promoting the repeal of the Act of Union and his difficult third album, *Freedom for All*. These 'monster gigs', which were held in various venues around the country, including Slane Castle in Meath, Croke Park in Dublin and Stradbally Hall, home of the Electric Picnic, showed the amount of popular support there was for Irish independence and for singer-songwriters of limited talent.

The impetus behind O'Connell grew and grew – until he cancelled a monster meeting in Clontarf in October 1843. The promoters claimed it was because he was 'tired and emotional', but everyone knew it was because the British said it couldn't go ahead.

## The Year of Dying Dangerously

If peace was running out of steam, that meant war could make a glorious comeback. The year 1848 had been designated the Official European Year of Revolutions, which meant that violent upheavals were all the rage across the continent. In Ireland a new group called Young Ireland joined the fun and said they were 'really looking forward to sorting the English out once and for all'. Unfortunately, the potato had already intervened and 1848 turned out to be a particularly useless year in which to do anything in Ireland, bar starve, emigrate or get into cannibalism, none of which was very appetising.

## Brotherhoods of Men

However, the seeds of revolt had been sown and the fight for Irish independence was gathering momentum. James Stephens, who had been inspired by his old mates Wolfe Tone and Robert Emmet, founded the Irish Republican Brotherhood (IRB) with the aim of setting up an independent Irish Republic 'by any means necessary', a phrase he borrowed from his other old mates, Jean-Paul Sartre and Malcolm X.

While Stephens was plotting in Europe, the Fenian Brotherhood was being formed in the US by Irish expatriates. Despite being driven from their homeland, they still wanted freedom for Ireland. However, when push came to shove, not very many of them actually wanted to leave their new lives in their new country.

Unfortunately, due to internal divisions, bad timing, poor organisation, rubbish weather, more unenthusiastic French people and possibly more rotten spuds, the Fenian Rising of 1867 wasn't a huge success. When Irish people woke up the next day, the English were still there.

## Home Rule Far from Home

While some were fighting for freedom, men such as Isaac Butt and Charles Stewart Parnell were taking the fight to Westminster, though not literally as the two of them wouldn't have stood a chance in London, especially with all those Beefeaters around. They were demanding Home Rule, which was the ludicrous idea that Ireland would be governed from Dublin. They sought to achieve this through peaceful means, such as talking for way too long, refusing to pay rent and being quite rude to English people. Parnell's Land League sought rights for put-upon tenants throughout Ireland and the British Prime Minister William Gladstone did seem keen to sort out the Irish Question, in much the same way as someone wants to sort out a headache.

While some progress was made, there was always someone who wasn't happy with the solution. That lack of happiness generally descended into recrimination and violence and then everyone sort of shrugged their shoulders and headed back to square one. Parnell even ended up in jail for his trouble, but eventually got out on a technicality. He and Gladstone then signed the Kilmainham Treaty, and Home Rule finally looked achievable ... until it all went pear-shaped again.

Then, in the most shocking event in Irish history, *The Tuppenny Tabloid* exclusively revealed that Parnell had slept with another bloke's wife. It even included detailed pencil drawings of the affair on pages 2–26. While that sort of carry-on might be fine in certain circles these days, this was Victorian Britain and it was a big no-no. And worse was to come. Back in Ireland, the Association of Devout Bishops Against Adultery, which was very much opposed to 'that kind of stuff', withdrew its support for Parnell. The game was up.

This was bad for Home Rule, bad for Kitty O'Shea's marriage and bad for Parnell. Once more the fight for Irish freedom had been ruined by the love of a good woman; not, of course, that it was her fault.

## Robert Emmet: Street-Fighting Man

There were plenty of idealistic young men and women who were willing to sacrifice their lives for the Irish cause. There were also plenty of others who were happy to go to university, drink too much and behave in the same way students had behaved since a young Plato was kicked out of the University of Ancient Greece for 'conduct unbecoming a future great philosopher'.

One Irish hero was Robert Emmet, a wealthy young Protestant chap from Dublin. In 1803 he led a rebellion on the streets of his native city against the British forces. He had carefully planned everything – and if 'everything' had gone according to that plan, it might have worked. Unfortunately, Robert had to rely on his student mates doing what they said they would and everyone knows you can't rely on students. In the end, fewer than 100 men showed up; all the others were out drinking or 'finishing an essay'. One, a certain Atticus O'Sweeney of the Dalkey O'Sweeneys, even claimed he didn't make it as his mother strictly forbade his participating in rebellions on weeknights. The brave Robert decided to give it a lash anyway; it wasn't the best idea he'd ever had.

**Student rebels were notoriously unreliable.**

The rebellion was easily crushed and Robert was arrested and tried for treason (the high kind). However, from the dock he made a speech which inspired generations of Irish rebels to come: 'When my country takes her place among the nations of the Earth, then and not till then, let my epitaph be written.' The English, who could be a petty lot at the best of times, buried him in an unmarked grave, so his epitaph would remain unwritten for a lot longer than he had intended.

# Top Five

## Irish People Who Became English Words

The word 'boycott' entered the English language after the land agent Captain Boycott found himself ostracised by the local community in the early 1880s because he simply did not like Irish people. But there are also plenty of real Irish people who have given words to the English language.

1) **Gob:** Daithí Ó Gub, a founding member of the Home Rule party, was the MP for Sligo Far East. He was famous for his obstructionist speeches in the House of Commons, one of which lasted nearly four years. When other MPs tried this tactic afterwards, the English would say: 'By Jove, that chap's got a bit of

a Gub upon him, wot.' This later became: 'The gob on yer man!'

**2) Galore:** Brendan and Mary-Patricia Galore from Clare won the Most Irish Catholic Couple in the World Award nine times between 1922 and 1936. Their main achievement was having forty-three children, all of whom were also Catholic. People would call them the Galore children, which then came to mean 'way too many' or 'lots of'.

**3) Kybosh:** Of Hungarian origin, the Kyboshes were a well-known family of undertakers in Cork. During the notorious Undertaker Wars of the 1950s, when Hanna von Kybosh was chief executive, they were accused of getting rid of every other undertaker in Munster in order to drum up business, thereby putting the 'kybosh' on the competition.

**4) Poitín:** In 1859 Seán Óg Mac An Phoitín discovered something that changed his life and the lives of so many others: you didn't have to spend money buying alcohol. Instead, you could make it at home using sugar and anything lying around the place, including soy sauce, grass and bits of old photocopier. Poitín can now refer to any domestically produced alcoholic drink with the power to make you blind.

**Sean Óg Mac An Phoitín is still with us in spirit.**

5) **Sleveen:** The rather debonair Finbarre Sleveen from Cavan was notorious in the 1930s. He married sixty-seven different women, set up 9,000 fake companies and pretended, at different times, to be a doctor, Winston Churchill, a seven-year-old girl, a small village in Romania and a bottle of very fine sherry. Anyone who met him usually ended up losing a lot of money, marrying him or both. After the experience, they would say: 'That Sleveen fella, well, I tell ya, he's some ... sleveen.'

# 10

# INDUSTRIAL WEAKNESS AND STRENGTH

## Land of Not Much Opportunity

While the rest of Europe was having fun fighting in the Industrial Revolution, the Irish, particularly in the southern part of the country, were too busy to get involved, as they were trying to earn a few quid so they could emigrate. Those in the northern part of the country, particularly around Belfast, did a fair bit more, though they did have some excellent natural resources there, including tons of linen, some very, very large ships and a famously strong work ethic. Southern Ireland didn't really need an Industrial Revolution as it didn't have much in the way of natural resources, such as oil, Chablis or even nuclear power. In fact, the only plentiful resources in the country were grass, sand, hummus and godliness, none of which was in big demand in Europe in the nineteenth century – and, technically speaking, hummus shouldn't even have been on the list.

In fairness, Ireland should really have had some valuable resources to offer the world in terms of beef, sheep and non-potato-based vegetables. However, the English took charge of all that produce and swore blind to the Irish that there was no real market for it abroad. The trusting Irish took them at their word on this, although there isn't really much choice when you have a cannon stuck in your face.

## From Country Cousins to City Slickers

The mainly rural population of Ireland had grown to about eight million by the time the Great Famine kicked in. However, starvation, emigration and the English had all done their utmost to reduce that figure. Of those who managed to survive and stay in Ireland, most had no choice but to move to the cities. They really didn't want to, as people from rural areas thought of urban types as uppity snobs. They considered them 'to be as bad as the Sassenach', as An t-Uasal Eoghan Gorm Rua Noir Mac An Gallivaun, head of the Union of Irish Country Folk, put it in his widely read pamphlet of 1864, *City People Give Me the Heebie-Jeebies!*

In truth, there was a lot of suspicion on both sides, as city folk looked on their country cousins as being 'more like hogs than humans', as Lord Sir Honorius Bryant-Queenslove III put it in his anti-peasant treatise of 1865, *Send the Bumpkins Home Now Before I Have Them All Bloody Shot!*

## Urban Sprawl

Life in the city was obviously very different from life in the countryside, apart from the overcrowding, the starvation and the lack of work, which were quite similar in both. People were forced to live on top of each other – and often literally in many cases.

Cities like Dublin, Cork, Limerick and Galway were inundated with people who had to live in huge slums or tenements. Often, there would be 300 or 400 families all living together in one small room. That room would be located in a house with about 200 or 300 small rooms, meaning that there could often be as many as

120,000 people living in one relatively small house. It was hardly the lap of luxury, though many folk at the time apparently claimed that while they may have been poor, they were happy. This has since been proven to be not true; they were, in fact, miserable.

## Working for the Man

These were hard times for working-class people, as they were called, though they were only called this on the rare occasions when they could find work. On a brighter note, however, it was great for employers, owners of factories and rich people in general. There were barely any labour laws to speak of, and exploitation of workers was encouraged and considered one of the very cornerstones of modern society. However, it was only a matter of time before someone was to ruin the party.

## Working against the Man

Back then, people were a lot simpler, and many didn't even know the difference between right and wrong. The only way to live appeared to be to divide society into owners and workers, powerful and powerless, rich and very, very poor.

However, men like James Connolly and Jim Larkin recognised that if they weren't going to be running their own factories and exploiting workers, they would have to fight on the other side. This struggle reached its apex in the Lockout of 1913, when employers in Dublin banded together to try to force their employees to literally work for peanuts and not to join unions.

The unions wanted all sorts of outlandish things for workers, such as civil rights, better working conditions and even payment in actual money.

The employers, who were led by William Martin Murphy, were quite forceful and enlisted the help of their dear friends in the police force to make sure the workers behaved themselves and didn't congregate to discuss how bad life was.

There were no real winners in the Lockout. The working people of Dublin not only starved even more but also got beaten up by the police for good measure. On the other side, the employers probably lost a few quid.

However, the Labour movement had been born and it ensured that Irish workers would never ever have to suffer again, whether through long hours, less pay or not having work at all.

If the struggle between workers and bosses and the fight for Home Rule had remained separate issues, Irish people might still be 'British' and working in their factories and supermarket chains for very little money. However, when those two struggles met for elevenses on Easter Monday 1916, the stage was set for real change.

**Sweeney Munitions:
a very equal opportunities employer.**

## Uniting the Workers

In the early years of the twentieth century, one large employer actually recognised the plight of his workers and tried
to involve them more in the running of his factory. Aurelio
Sweeney, who was one of the Rathgar Sweeneys, operated a
huge facility on the Military Road on the outskirts of Dublin
and was seen as a progressive and equal opportunities employer, not least by himself.

For example, Aurelio hired both men and women to do
the same jobs; it really didn't matter to him. He would also
hire farmer types, inner-city types and anybody who hadn't

yet been maimed by a workplace accident. There were also no age restrictions in his factory and even if you were eighty, you could still work for him right up until the day you died (though it was against factory rules to die while at work). In fact, even if you were just a child, you could probably have found a job in the Sweeney Munitions factory as long as you were tallish and strong enough.

Aurelio also allowed small teams of workers to run various departments in the factory, such as the Testing Department, the Explosives Division and the top-secret Chemical and Biological Warfare Development Laboratory, which even Aurelio himself didn't like visiting.

The Sweeney Profit-Sharing Scheme was considered to be ahead of its time both in Ireland and around the globe. It basically meant that if the factory was making a huge profit, the employees' salaries would also rise. So, for example, if an employee was getting a loaf of stale bread for his or her ninety hours a week, Aurelio would double it if the factory was making money. This was a handy arrangement, as he owned a nearby bread production facility, which employed nearly 2,000 people.

The Profit-Sharing Scheme was particularly beneficial for employees from 1914–1918 when the Sweeney Munitions factory was supplying weapons to all sides during the Great War. Unfortunately, when the dreaded peace came in 1918, a lot of employees lost a lot of money, as Aurelio obviously made them pay for the losses. 'Fair's fair,' he wrote in a telegram to his workers from his winter palace in the Bahamas. He had left Europe four years earlier as he wasn't all that keen on world wars.

# Top Five

## Irish Exports The World Can't Live Without

Being a small nation, Ireland never had the same resources as countries like Britain or Germany, so it couldn't really develop as a major manufacturing location or as an exporter. However, it did have certain indigenous industries and exported products like stout, crisps and biscuits, though only when there was a really huge surplus of all three.

1) **Peat:** One of the greatest economic developments for Ireland was when it discovered that bits of the ground could be burnt as fuel. Ireland was more or less covered in bits of ground, so the Irish could easily afford to export peat and other bits of bog to whoever would buy it.

2) **Rain:** You can either look on rain as something wet that falls from the sky or as a valuable resource. Ireland chose the latter option and has been exporting

more than sixty different types of rain to various countries around the globe since the ninth century. It is still the world's largest exporter of wet weather.

3) **People:** Apart from fresh air, leprechauns and ferns, the one thing Ireland always seemed to have too many of was people. Back in the 1840s, for example, the English had to do a huge cull as there were so many of them (see The Really Super Great Famine,

p. 88). From then on, Ireland has been regularly and efficiently exporting people to every single country on the planet, often whether they needed them or not.

4) **Chat:** There is nothing the Irish have more of than a bit of old chat, with many economists reckoning it to be their single most abundant resource. Wherever the Irish were exported to, they always brought chat with them and often tried to sell it to the locals. If they wouldn't buy any, they would just force it on them.

5) **Luck:** While it might seem slightly intangible as exportable produce goes, Ireland has always managed to trade on its luck in global markets. Indeed, when Irish charm and blarney ran out in the late 1950s, luck was all the Irish had left. They put it to good use internationally and the 'luck of the Irish' often trades at extremely high prices, particularly at race meetings in England.

# 11
# THE BIRTH OF THE CÚL

## Time To Get Cúl

Being subjugated by the Vikings, the Normans and the English for the best part of 1,000 years was not good for the Irish soul. It was quite difficult to hang onto one's Irishness when foreign types were forcing you to speak their language, play their faintly ridiculous sports and become as much like them as possible. Throw in the fact that the English also made it illegal to 'look or act in an Irish fashion' and it was a miracle the Irish had any culture left.

However, in the second half of the nineteenth century, things began to change. The Irish realised that the English way of life wasn't really doing it for them. Movements began to spring up all over the country that aimed to get people to embrace all the Irish traditions and pastimes that had been beaten out of them. It was time to revive Irish culture and make Ireland a happening nation once again. Irish people in the late nineteenth century knew they were 'cúl'; now they just had to show it.

## Hedging Their Bets

The first target for the country was the Irish language, the fiery tongue of the mighty Gaels, which had been used to repel the Romans, the Visigoths and, much later, a large group of rather nice Australian tourists who hadn't done anything wrong. The Irish had done their best to speak Viking, Norman and English but had never really been comfortable with any of them. Now they were determined to get their own language back.

The revival was driven by the Gaelic League, which encouraged people to speak Irish, look Irish and act Irish. Schoolchildren were encouraged to speak the old tongue through the shrewd and injudicious use of things like big sticks, leather straps and clips around the ear. Classes were held in or near hedges, though generally on the non-raining side of the hedge if one could be found. Hedges were used for two reasons: one, the teacher could use a bit of the hedge as a stick, and two, the Irish thought that the English wouldn't be smart enough to look for hedge schools behind hedges.

## In a Gaelic League of Their Own

The Gaelic League also commanded the nation's poets, novelists, playwrights, storytellers, gossips and barflies to use Irish whenever possible. It translated various words such as 'potato', 'cement' and 'ramps' into Gaelic as 'potáto', 'shemint' and 'rampaí'. From 1893 on, poets were ordered to include at least one of these words in every poem they wrote. This was met by a lot of opposition, with the Union of Sensitive Poets issuing a statement saying it restricted their expressiveness. The Gaelic League responded that if a nineteenth-century Irish poet couldn't get the word 'potáto' into a poem, they were hardly worthy of the name 'poet'.

**Writers were required to sprinkle fadas
throughout their work.**

Novelists were also asked to write their books in Irish or at the very least stick in a few Irish accents (or 'fadas' as the Gaelic League liked to call them) so they looked and sounded more authentically Irish. Playwrights were instructed to write plays that were related to typical Irish themes, such as oppression, emigration and death. Upbeat plays were outlawed and there was in fact no happy Irish play until Samuel Beckett wrote *Happy Days* in 1961. Oscar Wilde's plays didn't count 'for obvious reasons', as the Gaelic League put it in a secret memo. The memo was leaked in 1902 by GaeliLeaks, the anarchist group that used to expose any kind of anti-Irish shenanigans.

## Requited Love of Ireland

Of all the 'Irish' writers of the time, one stood out because of his great love of Irishness (and of Irish women who tended not to love him back). This was the great William Butler Yeats, who was named Ireland's Least Boring Poet a record thirty-six times. Just over 90 per cent of his poems are dedicated to a woman called Cathleen ní Houlihan, although no records can be found of her birth or death. In fact, she may have been just made up to represent Ireland, which is typical of the kind of stuff poets get up to when we're not looking.

Yeats was also a staunch supporter of the Irish revival and founded the Irish Literary Theatre along with Lady

Gregory. Later known as the Abbey, it staged many Irish plays in its early incarnation, including *When the Rain Fell and Just Didn't Stop*, *The Day All the Spuds Died* and *Begob Here Come the English Again*, as well as three of Yeats's lesser known musicals, *Marry Me Maud*, *Come Here to Me, Cathleen, You Fine Thing!* and *Don't Leave Me this Way, Cathy Dearest*.

**The musical plays of W. B. Yeats were very popular.**

### The Cult of Culture

There was no point having a cultural revival if Irish people were just going to sit at home and drink whiskey until they fell asleep in front of the fire. The plain people of Ireland were urged to take up traditional Gaelic pastimes such as fiddling, piping, line-dancing and doing impressions of the English. The local pub, church hall and 'cumann' became hubs for people to gather in and be Irish for a few hours every evening. Here, they would sing songs, tell stories and, when they got around to it, plot the overthrow of their English oppressors.

## A Sporting Chance

Sport was another area where the Irish had lost their way. The Vikings had them playing strange Scandinavian sports such as jumping into ice-cold water, shouting loudly and the ancient game of 'pillage and plunder'. Even worse, the English had made them play cricket. After several hundred years of that, it was no wonder the Irish wanted to have their own sports.

In 1884 Michael Cusack founded the Gaelic Athletic Association, the aim of which was to promote Irish sport. Unfortunately, the only sport they had at the time was running quite fast away from the English. This inspired Cusack to invent two new sports: Gaelic football, a clever mix of soccer and rugby, and hurling, a not-quite-as-clever mix of cricket and belting people over the head with a piece of wood. People were ordered to play these sports every Sunday or risk being sent to Coventry. This literally happened to the O'Shaughnessy family, who were exiled to England in

1893 and now own a huge amount of property in the Greater Coventry area.

The GAA also forbade the playing or watching of any English sports by Irish people and banned its members from speaking English, wearing Manchester United soccer shirts and kissing English people unless they were particularly attractive.

## Fighting to be Irish

As the Irish started becoming more Irish than even the Irish themselves, they grew very proud of their heritage. Indeed, the people were so happy to have their own culture that they often swore that they would defend it to the death – something that would come in very handy in the first two decades of the twentieth century.

## The Stanislaus Sweeney School of Method Irishness

The desire to be more 'Irish' was a crucial part of the national identity from the late nineteenth century on. Whether Protestant or Catholic, English-speaking or Gaeilgeoir, people were keen to assert their Irishness in whatever way possible.

A young man called Stanislaus Sweeney saw a gap in the market and believed he could teach people to act in a more Irish fashion. At first, only people who really needed these skills professionally, such as politicians, priests and Irish mothers, attended his classes. However, as his reputation grew, more and more ordinary people came to him and the Stanislaus Sweeney School of Method Irishness soon had operations all over Ireland.

Stanislaus told his students to say things in an Irish accent and litter their chat with crucial 'Irish' words, such as 'begorrah', 'fierce' and 'Jaysus'. He would give each of them little notebooks which contained English phrases that would make them sound really Irish without having to actually speak Irish. These included: 'It was far from [insert something posh here] you were reared', 'Would you go on outta that?' and 'Go on, so, another pint won't kill me'. He also taught them to dance with their arms held straight against their sides, to bang a drum-like instrument called a bodhrán and stay up very late talking about what a sad place Ireland was in the olden days.

While the school was a success for more than four decades, it was closed down when it was discovered that

Stanislaus was actually American and was only a very distant relation of the Connemara Sweeneys. He was last heard of working in Argentina teaching former Nazis how to be less German.

# Top Five

## Literary Lights You May Not Have Heard Of

Ireland has produced some literary giants in its time, including four Nobel Prize winners in William Butler Yeats, George Bernard Shaw, Samuel Beckett and Seamus Heaney. At least two others, Oscar Wilde and James Joyce, probably could have won it. But there are also other Irish literary stars who never won that prize or anything else and whose names have all but disappeared from the Irish literary scene.

1) **Breda:** Although completely illiterate, young Breda ní hÓige still managed to keep a diary of her life from the age of two right up until she died aged 143 in 1997. Seven volumes in length and written in an illegible mix of English, Gaelic, Sanskrit and Early Gibberish, it recounts every second of her miserable life, including being born, starving, working for a US software giant and dying of very old age.

**2) Arthur Jones O'Culley:** Though none of his plays has ever been staged, Jones O'Culley wrote 280 of them between 1910 and his death in 1953. His work chronicles human life on the Burren in a way that no one had ever bothered attempting before. Full of annoying phrases, stereotypes to beat the band and ridiculously implausible storylines, many of his best plays were, at best, not very good.

**3) Seán Óg Mac SeánieÓg:** A Donegal native, Mac SeánieÓg wrote some hugely important poems in the 1700s. Written exclusively in his very own version of Donegal Gaelic, his poems focused on every single hardship that the True Gaels ever suffered. His style has been described as being similar to Dante, though this is mainly because not one of his poems is shorter than the entire Divine Comedy.

**4) William Hurley:** Graduating from Trinity College Dublin in June 1934, Hurley left Ireland early next morning, living in Berlin and Madrid before making New York his home. He wrote in English and made no reference to his home country in any of his works. In fact, when asked by an interviewer in 1972 why he left Ireland, he replied: 'I'm not from Ireland. I swear. And if you print that I am, I'll hurt you.'

**5) Richard O'Hennessey:** While alcohol has ruined many a writing career, it was the making of Richard O'Hennessey's. An early drinker – he had his first pint when he was just three months old – O'Hennessey only wrote one novel, *The Beggar's Blanket*, 'a sprawling, often unintelligible masterpiece'. Critics have been quick to point out his main literary influence in the book: booze. The novel was unfinished at the time of his death and, though many attempts have been made, no one has yet finished reading it.

# 12

# A REALLY GREAT WAR

### Ready for Some Real Action

As the twentieth century broke upon the world, the fight for independence took on a new impetus as Irish people asserted their identities, rose up against the rich and powerful and decided that, after hundreds of years of rather tiresome oppression, enough really was enough. Talking their way out of trouble hadn't worked, so now it was time for action.

### War of the Worlds, Part 1

While Irish minds were focusing on booting the English out, another slightly less important conflict was brewing in Europe. The Germans were getting a bit above themselves and thought the continent would be better off if they ran it. It was not the last time they would think this, but on this occasion their domination of Europe was to remain a dream.

The Irish, sensing an opportunity in England's woes, decided to send one of their own men to the continent to lend a hand. Unfortunately, this young man, whose name was Gavin Pringle, got very drunk on absinthe and accidentally shot dead a little-known European leader called Archduke Franz Ferdinand. Gavin was so tipsy that he could hardly speak and ended up giving a slurred version of his name to the authorities when arrested. As a result, 'Gavrilo Princip' was blamed for the assassination, so thankfully Ireland's involvement in sparking the First World War and the next forty years of bloodshed remained a secret.

When the First World War started, the Irish obviously felt very guilty about starting the whole shooting match and wrote to the British Prime Minister,

Herbert H. Asquith, telling him that it was the moral duty of all the people on the islands of Ireland and Britain to get involved in the war.

'Europe needs us,' they wrote, though they obviously didn't mention their role in kicking it off. They also guaranteed that nobody in Ireland would do anything about the fight for independence until 'those damned Hun types have been sorted out once and for all'.

However, not everyone on the Irish side got that particular memo.

## Rising Time

After numerous ill-fated attempts to rise up and overcome the British, the Easter Rising of 1916 was, unfortunately, not a whole lot different. For starters, many of the Volunteers who were being relied upon by the rebel leaders to defeat the English had joined the British Army to fight against Germany, leaving a much-depleted force back home.

It was supposed to be a huge army of workers and revolutionaries, made up of the Irish Volunteers and the Irish Citizen Army, all willing to die for Ireland and rallying to Patrick Pearse's call that 'Ireland unfree shall never be at peace'. However, no one could fix a date or a time to have the Rising, as they all had commitments, including striking, taking the kids to school and looking for badly paid work.

**The Easter holidays proved a bad time to hold a rebellion.**

## Blue Monday

So, on Easter Monday 1916, only about seven people showed up for the revolution. (Note: the actual figure was probably about 1,200, though numbers sometimes just get in the way of good history.) As it was going to be hard to beat the British Army with so few Volunteers, they decided to occupy the General Post Office (GPO) on Dublin's O'Connell Street, as it was strategically important, unguarded and one of them had a set of keys. Interestingly, although there were only seven people there, all four million Irish people alive today, particularly after a few pints, claim their grandparents were in the building on that fateful day.

Having secured the GPO, the rebels proudly read out the 'Proclamation of the Irish Republic', though there were very few people around to hear it. It was Easter, so a lot of Dubliners had gone to Bray, Torremolinos and various other holiday hotspots around Europe. Those that couldn't afford to go on holidays had gone to the races at Fairyhouse or were watching the Great War on the History Channel.

Finally, some off-duty British soldiers walked by and raised the alarm. The GPO was surrounded and the British Army ordered the rebels out. However, they kept shouting: 'Not until you meet our demands: an Irish Republic, our own soccer team, a helicopter and some basic civil rights.' After a few days of this, the British went and shot them.

## Myths, Martyrs and a Major Mistake

The one thing the English had always been really good at in Ireland and in their other colonies around the world was shooting the natives dead. It was a policy that they had followed ruthlessly and which had never really backfired.

However, this time was a bit different and their

shooting of the rebel leaders turned out to be a big mistake. Until they did that, some Dubliners hadn't really noticed the Easter Rising, except that stamps and Lotto tickets had been difficult to get in the city centre. However, as soon as the British shot the 'boys in green' there was uproar. They became martyrs overnight and the Irish were very angry indeed. It didn't help that they shot them without giving them a fair trial and that in the case of James Connolly at least, also badly injured and strapped to a chair.

With the Germans giving it socks in Europe, the British were really not enjoying all the bloodshed as much as they traditionally had. Independence was getting ever closer for the fighting Irish.

## That Sinking Feeling

Mystery still surrounds the events of 15 April 1912 when the *Titanic* sank after leaving Ireland. Now, however, an eyewitness account reveals what really happened. Virgil Sweeney, an Irish 'poet' and Professor of Safe Ships at Stanford University, was on the *Titanic* that fateful night. His diaries reveal how the unsinkable was sunk:

> **April 14, 1912:** Having passed myself off as an expert on really big, really safe ships, it was no surprise that Captain Smith summoned me to a meeting on the bridge at about 11 p.m. He asked me what I knew about icebergs. I looked him straight in the eye, told him I wasn't a fan and said I much preferred the Wibbly Wobbly Wonder.
>
> 'Not Icebergers,' he barked. 'Icebergs.'
>
> 'Oh, icebergs,' I said. 'They're big, white and easy to spot, even in the dark.'
>
> 'Look around, Professor,' he said.
>
> I turned and looked. Sure enough, there was something very big and very white heading straight for us.
>
> 'It certainly has all the characteristics of your common-or-garden iceberg,' I said. 'If it's also very hard, I think we can safely say it's an iceberg. However, if it's soft and squishy, it might just be a very big marshmallow.'
>
> 'What I need to know,' Smith said, ignoring my

valiant attempt at levity, 'is what damage it will do.'

'Well, none if you can avoid hitting it, which is always the best option in situations like this,' I said, believing honesty was the best option.

'It's too late,' he shouted.

'I'm not a betting man, Captain,' I said, which wasn't strictly true, 'but right now I'd put my admittedly rather meagre life savings on that big chunk of ice sinking this big chunk of metal.'

'Don't be a fool!' he said. 'This is the *Titanic*.'

**April 15, 1912:** I am sitting in a small lifeboat floating in the middle of a big ocean. While I am usually more than happy to win a bet, it gives me no pleasure that the *Titanic* is nowhere to be seen. However, the iceberg is still floating around menacingly, no doubt looking for other unsinkable liners to demolish.

# Top Five

## Cult Films About Ireland
## You May Never See

There have been plenty of popular films made about Ireland, from old classics such as *The Commitments* and *The Field* to more modern ones like *King of the Travellers* and *Mrs Brown's Boys: D'Movie*. However, there have also been quite a few 'cult' films which are not that well known outside Ireland, though this could also be because they aren't very good. Here are five worth looking out for.

1) **Little Mickeleen Gets A Gun and Meets A Lovely Girl:** Made in 1924, this silent, black-and-white-and-rather-grainy epic is, at fourteen hours, one of the longest films ever made. It tells the true story of a poor farmhand who joins the Easter Rising, saves his family's farm from an evil landlord and gets engaged to his childhood sweetheart, Colleen, all during one eventful afternoon. When it is later revealed that her family is anti-republican, he is ordered to shoot her and her fourteen big brothers. Faced with this difficult task, he decides he wasn't that keen on her in the first place and instead marries Bridey, a local girl of very few morals and even fewer brothers.

2) **Erin Forever:** This blockbuster was shot in the corner of a Hollywood studio, with very big photographs of Ireland placed behind the actors to give the impression they were actually in the country. It tells the history of Ireland through the eyes of a small, red-haired girl called Little Orphan Erin. At the age of twelve, she converts to Christianity and is subsequently attacked by Vikings, seduced by

a debonair Englishman, starves when her potatoes get stolen, emigrates to the US, runs guns for the IRA, becomes a professional boxer, joins the police and eventually gets elected President of the USA. In the final scene she makes Ireland the 51st state of the union and everybody lives happily ever after.

**3) Freedom:** The Troubles in the North are the background for this rom-com, in which a handsome, wise-cracking terrorist meets a gorgeous double agent working for Britain's MI5. As they go about their daily lives, they fall in love and have great fun altogether, proving that love will flourish even in the midst of the most violent of armed struggles. Eventually, at their wedding, all sides in the North agree that love is much more important than conflict and the war ends – which is sort of what happened in real life, though not really.

**4) Begorrah, 'Tis Half-Pint Harry Himself:** This hilarious comedy focuses on the trials and tribulations of the eponymous Harry, who is half-Irish, half-leprechaun and all mouth. He wins the Lotto, says something funny about potatoes, drinks a lot, accidentally marries the Queen of England, loses the entire island of Ireland in a card game, says something funny about having red hair, manages to win

Ireland back at a horse race and then becomes a national hero. It is a madcap romp, full of the very best in lazy stereotypes, casual racism and stage Oirishness.

**5) The Rock:** In 1817 Finbarr O'Grady is given a rock by his dying grandfather and told he must never lose it. Unfortunately, Finbarr is a bit of a bowsy and throws the rock away a few minutes later. Fast-forward 160 years to 1977 and his distant cousin, Majella Creedon, trips over the same rock (or a very similar one) and breaks her pinkie. And so a family feud is born which will dominate the lives of every O'Grady and Creedon for centuries to come. This epic story will resonate with any family whose history has been affected by a carelessly cast rock.

# 13
# INDEPENDENCE DAZE

**Revolutionary leader Éamon de Valera loved being Irish ... most of the time.**

## The People Have Risen

When the English executed a nice bunch of local

boys for no other reason than they occupied a post office and demanded some basic human rights, their popularity plummeted to a new low. A poll in *The Revolutionary Times* from just after 1916 showed that a staggering 0 per cent of Irish people now wanted them to remain in power in Ireland.

The political party that capitalised on this was Sinn Féin, which had been founded in 1905 by Arthur Griffith, Bulmer Hobson, Scrumpy Jack Hornblower and Blowtorch Bacardi. Interestingly, Sinn Féin was the Irish for 'Brits Out', though Griffith and Hobson always told the English that it meant 'Loyal to the Crown'.

Following the euphoria of 1916, the party became slightly more interested in violence, which was good timing as violence was really the only show in town between 1916 and 1923. One of the main men from the Rising, an American chap called Ché 'Éamon' de Valera became its president in 1917. He had fought in the Rising, swearing to his fellow rebels that he was as Irish as they came.

However, when the English caught him and suggested that they might like to execute him, he cleverly remembered that he wasn't, in fact, Irish.

## Coming Home to Rule

In the 1918 general election, Sinn Féin won seventy-three seats, though they declined to take them as they weren't very comfortable and weren't even in Ireland. Sinn Féin then politely sent a telegram to Westminster saying they were not to worry about things as 'we are just going to form our own little government over here in Dublin'.

At the first 'Dáil' the delegates declared the formation of a new republic as laid out in the original Proclamation of the Irish Republic, although it has long been suspected that they added a few bits, including late shopping on Thursdays, full Irish breakfasts on weekend mornings and the continuation of all social welfare payments from Britain even after independence.

De Valera elected himself president and made his best friend, Michael Collins, the Minister for Terrorising the Brits. De Valera and Collins were to remain the best of pals forever ... or at least until they started trying to murder each other a few years later. That kind of thing can really damage even the most firm of friendships.

**War and More War**

However, despite the formation of the Dáil, not everyone was keen to give up the noble act of fighting in the name of freedom. Elements on both sides just really wanted to keep the war effort going and so just as peace was about to break out, the English and the Irish got together and decided to hold a War of Independence.

The Irish hired the Irish Republican Army (IRA)

under Collins to do its fighting. It was pretty small compared to the British Army, so Collins' plan was to assassinate all English people in Ireland one by one. Unfortunately, it was estimated that this could take up to a hundred years and no one has that kind of time, particularly in a war situation. So, using guerrilla warfare (though without gorillas) and flying columns (though without flying), the IRA attacked as many individuals as they could. Just before they finished them off, they would order them to tell their friends who had done it so they would get scared and leave the country. Apart from that one major flaw, it was a flawless plan.

## How To Get Black and Tanned

However, if there is one thing the British don't like to be outdone in, apart from badminton, tea-drinking and train-spotting, it's dealing with restless natives. So they put an ad in *The Pits of London* under the heading 'Get a Mick, Earn a Crust' which offered 'work to anybody who wants to shoot some paddies. No rules except: THE MORE YOU GET, THE MORE YOU EARN!'

Thousands applied, either because they hated the Irish or were just bored since the First World War had ended so tragically early for them. These men, who were called Black and Tans, tried to out-IRA the IRA, which really required some effort. As their commanding officer, Lt Col Billy 'Razor' 'Pitbull' 'Tommy the Tank' Thompson told them in his now famous recruitment speech: 'They pull a knife, you pull a gun. They send one of yours to the hospital, you send one of theirs to the morgue. They shoot an RIC man, you shoot every single person in some random, unrelated village.' Thompson was later court-martialled for stealing the speech from the Hollywood film *The Untouchables*.

Then, in November 1920, the IRA went too far ... which naturally led to the others going even further. On a day that will be forever known as Bloody Sunday (along with more than 1,600 other famous Bloody Sundays in Irish history), the RIC Auxiliaries shot dead fourteen random people watching a Gaelic football match in Croke Park. Which was generally recognised as not being very sporting of them.

## Treaty Time

Like a lot of other wars in history, it turned out that the War of Independence wasn't that much fun, involving as it did a lot of violence, bloodshed and death. Sooner or later, everyone was bound to get bored and start looking for a peaceful solution. This came in the form of a truce which was signed in 1921.

This led to de Valera sending a delegation to London to negotiate a treaty with the British, though he didn't go himself as he had 'a bit of a headache'. In London, Collins was one of those who signed the Anglo-Irish Treaty, which created the Irish Free State. Unfortunately, he later claimed that he also accidentally signed his own death warrant, which Lloyd George may have carelessly left lying on his desk.

At the historic moment when the Treaty was signed, a young MP called Winston Churchill was heard to say: 'Well, I bet that's the end of conflict in Ireland for some time, maybe even forever.'

## Not Very Civil War

When Collins, Griffith and the other Irish representatives arrived back in Dublin, they had hoped for a huge civic reception at the airport, with a brass band and banners, followed by an open-top bus parade around the country. What they got was a very, very angry de Valera, though miraculously his headache had completely disappeared.

A vote took place in the Dáil on whether to accept the Treaty or not. It was a tough choice, as accepting it meant a big civil war, while rejecting it meant they would start being shot at by the nasty British mercenaries all over again. The former won the day, the Treaty was approved and as expected, de Valera lost the rag and resigned. The Irish then started the Civil War, which was a pleasant change from the Easter Rising, the First World War and the War of Independence, though equally violent, bloody and uncivil.

Like all the best civil wars, the Irish one was particularly nasty, pitting Irishman against Irishman, brother against brother, sister against that 'complete cow from number 16'. It was also very hard to tell whose side everyone was on, which meant sometimes you just had to shoot people and hope they were your enemies. One man from Killygobber even shot himself dead, thinking he was spying for the other side. It later turned out that he was a spy, so he was dead right to shoot himself.

Eventually most people realised that civil wars, in which you were actually expected to fight against family members, friends and neighbours, were even more stupid than your common-or-garden ones. In 1923, while a sizable portion of the population still remained alive, the Civil War ended.

**Mystery still surrounds the shooting of Michael Collins.**

# Michael Collins:
## The Brazilian Connection

One of the most infamous moments of the Civil War was the assassination of General Michael Collins. Known as 'Ireland's answer to Michael Collins', he was worshipped by people far and wide. However, a lot of mystery surrounds his death to this day. Was he murdered in an ambush in Béal na mBláth by anti-Treaty IRA forces? Or was he shot by a lone gunman from the sixth floor of the Béal na mBláth Book Depository? And was that lone gunman actually Éamon de Valera?

Well, one part of the mystery can now be solved. A snippet of a letter written in Brazil by explorer Tarquin Livingstone Sweeney of the Fermanagh Sweeneys contains a stunning revelation:

> I had only said 'Take me to your leader' as a joke, but the tiny Mjawi people had absolutely no sense of humour. They led me to a hut, which was at least three times the height of all the other huts and could only have been built for a taller man. The tribes people shouted and pointed at the hut: 'Bigfella! Bigfella! Bigfella!'
>
> I suddenly realised they were telling me that legendary Irish leader Michael Collins – the Big Fellow – lived in the hut and had somehow convinced them that he was a god and should be their leader. Collins must have faked his own death in order to

escape de Valera's evil clutches and ended up in Brazil. Genius!

I held my breath as the hut door opened. Then out he walked: a Mjawi man at least six inches shorter than any other man there. The Mjawi people then all burst out laughing. Perhaps I had underestimated their sense of fun and their knowledge of recent Irish history. But perhaps more importantly, it meant Michael Collins had been shot dead after all.

# Top Five

## Smallest Battles That Nearly Changed Irish History

War is an integral and exciting part of any country's history and this is no less true of Ireland. Along with the Easter Rising, the War of Independence and the Civil War, there have been some really great Irish battles. However, they don't always get mentioned, except perhaps in the footnotes to the appendix of the index of the unpublished ninth edition of *The Irish Journal of Forgotten Skirmishes*.

1) **The Battle of Rosslare:** In 54 BCE, Julius Caesar sent a fleet of his best marines to conquer Ireland. They

landed in Rosslare, but were immediately met by some very angry Hibernians and some very cold rain. They might have been Caesar's best, but those summer-loving Italians were no match for the Irish climate.

**2) The Siege of Sicla Gap:** One Irishman managed to fight off more than 10,000 Vikings in this famous siege, as he sought to protect his nine lovely daughters from the charming Scandinavians. Malachy Mc-Cormick won himself the title of toughest man in Connacht and when the British Army tried to take his homestead many centuries later, he also kept them out. In fact, rather unbelievably, McCormick is still holding out today, even though all of his daughters left for England some time in the thirteenth century.

**3) The Siege of Ballyticky:** In the small Wexford village of Ballyticky, the townspeople vowed that Oliver Cromwell would not pass. Every man, woman and child gathered together whatever weapons they could find, from muskets down to pieces of uncooked pasta, and waited for their destiny. He arrived and put everyone to the sword in less than seventeen minutes, beating his own previous world record.

**Was this to be Oliver Cromwell's last stand?**

4) **The Potato War of 1847:** It started simply enough: a rather hungry and angry Irishwoman threw a spud at a British soldier. He threw it back. Four days later, 800,000 Irish people, 60,000 British troops and 1,000 tonnes of potatoes lay dead. It really was the last thing Ireland needed in the middle of a famine, particularly a potato one.

5) **The St Patrick's Day Rising:** This took place in 1916 just one month before the Easter Rising, though it was considerably less successful. Some 2,000

Volunteers showed up, but they decided to have a quick pint before the revolution started. One thing led to another and that led to a few more and before they knew it, they were telling each other how much they loved the English. Next morning, after a big fry-up, they decided to try again at Easter.

# 14
# A NOT SO FREE STATE

## A Little Bit of Peace

After the tumultuous period between 1916 and 1923, nearly everyone on the island agreed that they should 'give peace a chance', at least for a few years. It was a nervous time for the Irish, however, as no one had ever run their own country before. They had put an ad in *International Recruitment* looking for someone with the right experience, but only one person replied and he had clearly made up a lot of things on his CV. For example, he had put 'Ran Ireland, 1700–1850' on it, when everyone knew the English had been in charge for those years (and hadn't even done a job worth boasting about).

Nonetheless, it was a time to rebuild and a time to work together for a better future. People were optimistic about things for the first time in more than 1,500 years and everyone on the island felt glad to be an independent, peaceful and united nation once again. Everyone that is apart from a few people living in the northern 'half' of the country.

## Divided We Stand

The Government of Ireland Act of 1920 had cleverly divided the island of Ireland in two. The twenty-six counties in the south were to have Home Rule, while the six in the north could do whatever they wanted, except become Communists, move to the Middle East or merge with Argentina.

The people in the north were not at all keen on being part of the Irish Free State. At the same time, they didn't want to go back to their homes in Britain, as some of them had left them many centuries previously and were worried that other people might now be living in them.

To sort this out, the Boundary Commission was established to finally divide Ireland along cultural, religious and economic lines, but always bearing in mind that the last thing anybody wanted was more bloodshed.

The commission looked at all thirty-two counties again, but decided that six for Protestants and loyalists who didn't want to be 'Irish' was just right. While a lot of people in the other twenty-six counties were obviously quite hurt about this, there were actually a few people in the six 'chosen' ones who were hurt that they *did* make the cut. Still, most people involved were confident that these so-called 'republicans' in the north wouldn't kick up too much of a fuss about it.

## A Time to Party

The first general election in the Irish Free State took place in 1923 and was won by new party Cumann na nGaedheal (or 'Come On The Irish'). Led by William Cosgrave, it wanted to leave behind the legacy of bloodshed and instead promote all kinds of modern ideas like job creation, economic growth and social welfare.

Éamon de Valera's Sinn Féin also won a number of seats, but again refused to take them. This time they claimed the ones in Dublin weren't the right colour, but everybody knew it was because Dev didn't want to take the oath of allegiance. The oath contained a pledge to be faithful to King George, to use phrases like 'By Jove' and 'Golly' a lot and to watch English soap operas every Sunday afternoon.

De Valera then decided that Sinn Féin was just too militaristic for him, so he set up his own party called the Soldiers of Destiny, though he used the Irish translation, Fianna Fáil, so no one would understand the military connotations. In 1927 the party won a bunch of seats, which they finally sat in. From photographs (and cartoons) of the time, you can clearly see that de Valera has his fingers crossed behind his back when taking the oath, thereby rendering it meaningless in the eyes of God and, more importantly, in his own eyes.

In the 1932 general election Fianna Fáil secured a majority and formed the government, with de Valera naming himself Supreme Leader For All Eternity of All Ireland Except The Northern Bits – or 'Taoiseach' in Irish. The first thing he did was to abolish the oath of allegiance. He also tried to abolish Cumann na nGaedheal and all of his enemies.

**De Valera didn't mind taking the oath of allegiance.**

### New Ireland

The new Ireland of the late 1920s and 1930s was a place full of freedom and hope. Culture blossomed, literature was in full swing and the people were happier than they had ever been before. It was felt that this was the time for the Irish to shine and to take their rightful place among the nations of the world. Nothing – absolutely nothing – could ruin this for the much put-upon Gaels. Except maybe the rise of fascism, an overbearing Catholic Church, a global recession and a new world war. But, realistically, there was little chance of any of those things happening in the 1930s. (Note: predicting history might look easy, but it is for professionals only; please do not try it at home.)

## The One and Only Church of Ireland

The rise of the Catholic Church took place under the watchful eyes of Archbishop John Charles McQuaid, who was more religious than the pope or even Jesus himself. It was even rumoured that he had actually met God on several occasions. He also knew all there was to know about sins, even though he had never committed one himself. He and de Valera wanted 'to make Ireland the holiest place in the known universe' and they worked very hard to achieve it. They even introduced prohibition to Ireland on 10 May 1934, though a violent backlash against it saw them repeal it just after lunch.

Still, this didn't deter the two men from their mission, and the ordinary Irish people were to enjoy and/or endure many years of some of the best Catholicism going.

## Global Recession? World War? No Way!

Ireland struggled to make up economic ground throughout the 1920s. However, in October 1929 a report from the Department of Finance revealed that things were finally going quite well and that Ireland could look forward to a more profitable decade in the 1930s 'barring some cataclysmic stock market event that destabilises the global economy or, worse, a world war. However, we don't see either of those events happening and anyway we're heading off for pints.'

Unfortunately, the Wall Street Crash of 1929 proved that first prediction just a tad wrong. Meanwhile in Germany, at around the same time, a rather psychotic young politician was planning major changes for the world, changes that would prove the other prediction even more wrong.

### A Brisk Constitution

The Constitution of Ireland, or *Bunreachtus na hÉireann* to give it its proper Latin name, came into force in 1939 and replaced the Danish one imposed by the Vikings in 876. The new one was originally written in Cuban by Éamon de Valera, as he didn't want any men or comely maidens to know exactly what he had planned for them. He then secretly passed it to Archbishop McQuaid while pretending to confess his sins in the Pro-Cathedral. The archbishop translated it into Latin and added some rules of his own. He also took out any references to kissing, women's undergarments and television that Dev may have slipped in by mistake or for a laugh.

It was then given to Deuteronomy 'Suilamhain' Ó Sweeney, an unemployable eighty-seven-year-old fisherman from Finglas, who translated it into Irish or as close to Irish as he could get. This was the 1930s and Irish was still very thin on the ground, so no one would be likely to understand or challenge it.

It was then submitted to the Vatican which had it translated into Aramaic. Finally, worn out and exhausted by its travels, the constitution returned to Ireland where, after a short stay in the Gresham Hotel, it was translated into English.

The constitution defined to the Irish people what it really meant to be Irish:

> We, the Irish people, assert our God-given right to not be British or English. Or Scottish or Welsh for that matter, though we are Northern Irish. Well, some of us are. We love and fear God, as long as He remains Catholic, and we only speak the language of the Gael (and English now and again). We are also fond of the spud, the booze and the bit of fighting. We are great at sport, namely the football (not the soccer!) and the hurling, and it is the solemn duty of every Gael (and his womenfolk) to get really good at those sports so when the rest of the world starts playing them we can beat them, because you'll never beat the Irish. We also

assert our God-given right to rule our own land and solemnly swear that our state shall be forever sovereign, independent and democratic – unless, of course, we're completely broke and need to sell it. Amen.

**The Irish Constitution was almost as holy as the Bible.**

# Top Five

## Republican Splinter Groups Who Didn't Make the Charts

The playwright and former IRA member Brendan Behan said that the first item on the agenda of any Irish republican meeting was the split. He wasn't far wrong and both the IRA and Sinn Féin have divided more times than the most divisive amoeba in the history of dividing single-cell organisms. From the original Sinn Féin came Fianna Fáil, Republican Sinn Féin and I Can't Believe It's Not Sinn Féin, while the IRA became, amongst others, the Provisional IRA, the INLA and the Real Provisional Unofficial Continuity IRA, which only formed late yesterday evening.

1) **Official Provisional Republican Sinn Féin:** This party was basically for anyone who wasn't sure which Sinn Féin they should be in, as it covered all bases. They simply opposed everything the real Sinn Féin ever said without necessarily knowing what it was ... unless, of course, their deadliest enemies in Very Unofficial Sinn Féin had opposed it first.

2) **The New 'Old' IRA:** While many considered the Old IRA and the New IRA to be terrorists, the New 'Old' IRA considered themselves to be gentlemanly freedom fighters. It is also important to remember that the New 'Old' IRA is not the same as the 'New' Old IRA.

3) **The Real IRA But Not The Other 'Real' IRA:** This is where it gets confusing, as the Real IRA But Not The Other 'Real' IRA will always tell you they don't even exist, which is bloody typical of them.

4) **Army of the Irish Republic (AIR):** Unfortunately,

no one ever really took AIR seriously as its acronym made it sound a bit silly. However, when it eventually split into Provisional and Official divisions, both groups became extra violent just because no one had taken their names seriously.

5) **The Splinters:** this little-known republican movement wasn't actually a republican movement at all, but a well-known showband working Ireland in the 1970s. They had several very minor hits, including 'Let's Be United as One', 'Come Live on the Border of My Love' and 'Your Mind Might Be Loyalist But I'm Going To Be Loyalest to Your Body'.

# 15

# ANOTHER WORLD WAR?
# NOT FOR US, THANKS

**A Great Decade for Fascists, if No One Else**

If you were a fascist, totalitarian maniac, Europe was the place to be in the 1930s. Franco in Spain, Mussolini in Italy and Hitler in Germany all managed to have great decades. Even in Ireland there had been the Blueshirts, a fascist group who modelled themselves on Italy's Blackshirts, the only difference being the Irish ones got the shirt colour completely wrong.

As most people know by now, Adolf Hitler was a particularly nasty piece of work and apparently wanted nothing less than to conquer the entire universe. He was also more than willing to annihilate anyone who got in the way of that dream. Then again, he also dreamed of being taller, blonder and more attractive to women. However, dreams don't always come true, a harsh lesson which the young Adolf was to learn later in life, though many people wished he had learned it a lot earlier.

However, as the winds of war prepared to sweep

across the globe, each and every man was going to have to stand up and fight for the freedoms that we all hold so dear. Except perhaps Éamon de Valera.

## The World at War

When Britain declared war on Germany, the nations of Europe knew they had no alternative but to choose sides. Ireland would have automatically had to fight alongside Britain if de Valera had not included a crucial clause in the constitution. It stated: 'Ireland will no longer be in the Commonwealth and if Britain is reckless enough to get involved in any more global conflicts, it needn't expect me to jump in.' This was a very smart move, as no one really wanted to fight the Nazis, who were a pretty ruthless outfit. After all, they weren't called Nazis for their love of daisies, crocheting and letting people live.

So when the war started, British Prime Minister Neville Chamberlain phoned Dev and told him all the details: when it would start, who to bring, what to wear, etc. However, de Valera broke it to him gently that Ireland wouldn't be going along, though he added that it was really lovely to get invited.

Later, the more persuasive new Prime Minister Winston Churchill also tried to convince Dev to join the war, but to no avail as Dev said the Irish had just converted to pacifism after several thousand years of rather pointless fighting.

The only worry for Churchill was whether Ireland might consider joining the Nazis. After all, if you couldn't beat the Nazis – and at this stage, it looked unlikely that anyone could – you might as well join them. De Valera knew that Hitler would love to have Ireland on board for the war, as it would give him access to Ireland, with its strategic ports, tasty pork sausages and real wool Aran sweaters.

However, Dev was no fool and trusted Hitler about as far as he could throw him. Actually, it was a bit less than that, because he could have thrown Hitler quite far, particularly if he used the same method as the hammer-throwers in the Olympics do.

## It's an Emergency

When the Second World War started, Ireland issued a statement saying it was neutral, but that it hoped for a fair fight and that the best country won. De Valera also shrewdly used the war to advance his own aims, introducing the Dev Emergency Act in 1939. The most pertinent part of the legislation read as follows:

> 'Because of the war, we have had to make one great man the outright leader of the country. This really fine fellow shall be obeyed by one and all. In other words, he is an all-powerful dictator, though not in the bad sense of the word. He will have various superpowers which he can use if he thinks it is in the best interests of the country to do so or even if he just feels like it. If anyone has a problem with this act, please go to Kilmainham Gaol immediately, where all of your complaints will be dealt with.'

The superpowers referred to in the act apparently included yogic flying, bi-location and the power to lock up anybody who disagreed with him. Interestingly, in the general election of 1943, Fianna Fáil won 100 per cent of the vote, so the Emergency superpowers obviously worked.

**Many essential items were hard to come by during the war.**

## The Rational Approach

The other part of the Emergency was that rationing was introduced. As most other European nations were busy fighting each other, imports of crucial products were not making it to Ireland. This meant there were shortages of prosciutto, tzatziki and cheap Spanish red wine. The Irish tried to be understanding about all this, though with these shortages there must have been times when it felt to them as if 'this war will never end'.

The war also led to a growth in emigration to Britain. As its workers were all away in Europe from 1939 to 1945 getting shot at and what-not, there were plenty of vacancies, so the Irish took their jobs – but in a nice, giving way. They also presumably took their women, but made sure to hand them back when the war ended.

## This is the End

De Valera managed to stay on friendly terms with both sides during the war. He even asked Hitler over for tea, though he was apparently too busy having his ass kicked on the Russian front to answer. But as the war dragged on, it began to look as if the Allies were going to win. Dev then started making all the right noises from the sidelines, shouting things like, 'Come on the good guys!', 'You'll never beat the British!' and 'Whistle while you work, Hitler is a twerp!'

Then, on the morning of 8 May 1945, de Valera sent Churchill a telegram: 'Winnie. Stop. Regret not being involved in war sooner. Stop. Will send troops now. Stop. Where are you guys? Stop.'

It is not recorded how Churchill responded or if he even got the message, for that very afternoon Germany surrendered and the war was over. As de Valera quipped to Archbishop McQuaid over pints in Jammet's that evening: 'In war, as in peace, timing is everything.'

## Black Market Blues

The people of Ireland had hoped that independence and the free market economy would bring them untold wealth. Unfortunately, all they got was the Great Depression and the Second World War, neither of which was conducive to consumerism. The 1930s were bad enough, but the problem really began to bite from 1939 on, when the war meant severe rationing. During this time, some people said they even missed the Great Famine, when at least you got to share a spud.

However, there were others who sought to solve this problem through altruism, entrepreneurship and flogging stuff on the black market. One such person was Victoria

Sweeney of the West Cork Sweeneys. She started life as a small entrepreneur in West Cork, flogging snuff, stuff that looked like snuff and stuff that bore no resemblance to snuff except that she had written 'This Is Snuff' on the label.

She didn't make a fortune from this, as the number of fatalities blamed on her snuff products precluded the business from expanding. However, she did make enough to open Victoria Sweeney's Black Market Emporium in Cork city. Although highly illegal, the gardaí turned a blind eye to it, as they were some of her best customers. The Emporium sold anything immoral that had been banned by Éamon de Valera's constitution, including transistor radios, alcopops, copies of *Ulysses* and car magazines that carried pictures of ladies with very few clothes on. It also sold things that couldn't be got because of the war, such as Dom Pérignon 1921, apple strudel, spaghetti bolognese and Panzer IV German tanks.

Victoria's business grew and she opened branches in Limerick, Tuam, Dublin, Termonfeckin and Belfast, always staying one step ahead of the law and the Catholic Church, as they remained her best customers. She had vowed to give up the black market once the war ended, but didn't as business was booming. However, in 1948 she mysteriously disappeared. She was seen for the last time by one of her assistants having a heated argument on the phone, which ended when she said: 'Are you threatening me, Your Archbishopness?'

# Top Five

## Emigration Hotspots for the Wandering Irish

Despite their great love of their own country, the Irish have been emigrating in their droves for millions of years. There have been many reasons for this, including the lack of jobs, a desire to enjoy sunshine and, of course, the English. But where did they go, what did they do there and how happy were the people in their new destinations to see them?

1) **England:** Millions of Irish went to live in England because the English were always so welcoming – but mainly because it was so close. While there, the English mainly gave the Irish jobs as builders, bombers, TV presenters, drunks, tramps and stage Irishmen.

2) **The US:** The United States has also welcomed millions of Irish to its shores over the years. They suffered a lot of prejudice when they first arrived, though black slaves arriving from Africa did them a favour and took their place in the prejudice marketplace. The main industries the Irish got involved with in the US were crime (prevention), nursing and crime (creation).

**3) Australia:** Before any Irish people emigrated to Australia, the English used to send Irish criminals there. This was obviously a huge number of people, as the English generally considered all Irish people to be innately criminal. However, in more recent times, Irish people have opted to go there. The Irish in Australia mainly work in areas such as barbecuing, getting sunburnt and drinking very strong lager.

**4) South America:** This was another popular destination during the 1800s, though the Irish were horrified to find that other Europeans had arrived before them. Most South American countries were delighted to welcome the Irish as they were much more friendly than the Spanish and Portuguese had been. The Irish mainly found work as conquistadores, freedom fighters and gougers (or 'gauchos').

**5) China:** During the global recession of 2008 to 2014, a plan was hatched by the Irish government for the entire population to emigrate to China. They were going to abandon Ireland, which had no money, no jobs and no prospects, and all four million or so people were going to slip into China quietly and live unnoticed among the 1.35 billion natives. They hope to have finally completed the move by the end of this year.

# 16
# SWINGING IN THE NEW REPUBLIC

## The Post-War Blues

The Second World War had provided huge excitement for the whole planet, but there was always going to be a comedown when it was over. This was true for all countries, but perhaps even more so for those which hadn't bothered getting involved. In the years after 1945, Ireland became isolated, lonely and even a little depressed. It felt unloved and even considered handing itself back to Britain or moving lock, stock and barrel to the US.

John Costello's Fine Gael party had also managed to displace Fianna Fáil, though it had done so by cleverly adopting the exact same policies as its bitter rival. The only difference between the two parties now was that one had been anti-Treaty and the other pro-Treaty back in the 1920s. Interestingly, no one in either party could remember which side they had been on, not that it mattered that much.

## The Not So Fab 1950s

What did matter in the 1950s was that, after all the doom and gloom of the late 1940s, there was even more doom and gloom to come in the next decade. This was mainly due to economic issues, as Ireland was yet again completely and utterly broke. There were only about 200 decent jobs in the whole country, which was never really going to be enough for the three million or so people looking for work.

However, the government did come up with the same brilliant solution as always for dealing with this problem. Called 'emigration', it basically meant that if you were Irish and couldn't find work in your own country, you could leave. This didn't just apply to men and women; the government also encouraged children to emigrate, offering them lollipops, orange cordial and a free cuddly toy with every one-way airline ticket purchased. The policy worked and the population dropped rapidly. Unfortunately, no one seemed happier; there were just fewer sad people.

## It's All There – but in Black and White

The mood in the country wasn't helped by the fact that everything was still in black and white in the 1950s, as Ireland couldn't afford to go colour until it joined the EEC in 1973. Typically, the Catholic Church did nothing to lighten the mood by banning comic books, ice-cream and smiling, and constantly reminding everyone that they were sinners and would end up in Hell.

**Ireland couldn't afford colour until 1973.**

The decade ended with Éamon de Valera making himself a saint and President for All Eternity at the ripe old age of 182. In a way, this marked the end of an era for Ireland, as Dev reminded people of the past and most people wanted to look forward, even if they thought there wasn't that much to look forward to. But there was, for it was time to replace the swinging cuts of the 1950s with the swinging struts of the 1960s.

**This Plan had better Work**

With a new Taoiseach in Seán Lemass, it was now time for Ireland to get working. The government introduced radical new policies that actually encouraged people to set up businesses. And it wasn't just Irish people. Foreigners were also encouraged to come to Ireland to build factories and exploit the workers. This was historic for Ireland, as it had spent the best part of 1,500 years trying to keep enterprising foreigners out of the country.

**Getting into the Swing of Things – or Not**

With the economy growing and people happy for the first time since St Patrick converted them, Ireland was set to join the cultural revolution that was sweeping the globe. Worldwide, the 1960s were going to be about young people, about freedom of expression and about doing what you wanted to do, not what you were told to do. People everywhere were going to embrace popular music, colourful trousers, hallucinogenic drugs and free love. It was the 'swinging sixties' and no one was going to get left behind. No one!

**Except the Irish …**

In March 1964 the Catholic Church issued the following statement:

There will be absolutely no 'swinging' in this country.

Anyone caught 'swinging', dancing or engaging in any similar activity will be condemned to an eternity in Hell. Love is also to stay unfree and trousers will remain of the black or grey variety. Young men will not look at young women and think to themselves: 'Gosh, I fancy some of that later.' Young women will continue to remain virgins until their wedding night and will regard sex as a functional thing only to be used for the production of more Irish sinners. Finally, there will be no summer of love in Ireland.

In fact, we will not be having autumns, winters or springs of love either. Love is evil. Many thanks and see you all on Sunday.

This was met with a collective groan by the people, which made the priestly part of the population quite angry. They stressed that the whole 'free love' thing was quite messy and was much more suited to your foreign types. Little did the priests know that in just a few years, when it joined the EEC in 1973, Ireland itself was to become a foreign country.

## Shock and Awe

The assassination of John Fitzgerald Kennedy in Dallas in November 1963 by Lee Harvey Oswald and various other individuals and organisations acting alone and together sent shockwaves around the world. Nowhere was the shock more felt than in Ireland, where JFK had been born and raised. (Note: JFK wasn't actually born or raised in Ireland.) He was young, handsome, Irish, successful and the most powerful man on the planet (though obviously not quite as powerful as the people who had him shot). He had also offered hope to millions of people in Ireland, hope that the world could be a better place, hope that the old ways were becoming obsolete and hope that bright, young men would lead us all into a brave new world (and not get shot dead).

In Ireland every single person remembers exactly where they were when they heard the news about JFK. For example, Fr Seán Óg Potterton, a parish priest from Co. Clare, recalls the impact it had on his life: 'Yes, it was a very weird time. I remember I had just dropped a tab of acid for the first time and was completely tripping. Then the housekeeper told me what had happened to JFK, but as she was tripping too, I didn't believe her. We moved to Goa about three weeks after that.'

Sarah Flynn-Stone from Tralee in Co. Kerry also has strong memories of the day: 'I was crying non-stop. It was the saddest thing ever, yet in many ways it was also a really happy occasion. Or am I thinking of when Prince Charles married Lady Diana? I always get those two days mixed up.'

Rufus MacSweeney of the Las Vegas MacSweeneys remembers exactly where he was too: 'Believe it or not, I was actually in Dallas that very afternoon. I was on a grassy knoll near where the president's car was passing and had just pulled my Glock out when all hell broke loose. There was screaming, shouting and lots of confusion. It was terrifying. It wasn't until I woke up back in my hotel room three days later that I even realised he was dead. Luckily, I was pretty sure I wasn't.'

# Top Five

## Irish Rockers and Rollers Who Weren't Top of the Pops

From the 1960s on, Ireland produced some of the finest singers and groups around, despite the fact that non-God-related music was illegal until 1976. From rock bands like Thin Lizzy and the Boomtown Rats to pop acts like U2 and Westlife, and from singers like Dana and Enya to modern rockers like Sinead O'Connor and Daniel O'Donnell, the Irish have always been at the forefront of the world music scene, though not all have enjoyed mega international success.

1) **Breege:** From somewhere mystical in the westest part of the west of Ireland, Breege was born Brigid O'Shaughnessy, but felt a one-word name was the surest way to success. She recorded sixty-two albums, the most popular of which was *Light Dancing God Clouds*. It featured one song, called 'Light Dancing God Clouds', which went on for ninety-four minutes and consisted of Breege chanting these four words while several cats purred in the background. The album sold nineteen million copies in Turkey.

2) **Fr Fintan Tierney:** He was one of the few priests to make it on the international rock scene and his actions were only forgiven by the Catholic Church in Ireland as 'he was almost as famous as Jesus'. His act was, however, a lot more suggestive and lewd than Jesus'. For example, he invented the Tierney Thrust, though it was edited out when he tried it at PriestFest in the summer of 1985. His biggest hit was 'I Wanna Be Your Lovin' God'.

3) **Sea of Druids:** This prog rock band was unique in that all nine members sang lead vocals and played lead guitar. Each also insisted on playing their own solos in each song, meaning their concerts could last for up to three weeks. All of their songs were

based around Irish history, including their biggest hit, 'The History of Ireland from 4000 BCE to The Arrival of Christianity'.

**4) The Irish Sons of Bitches:** Mixing republicanism, God, sex, anger, traditional music, pills and violence might have seemed like a bad idea to some, but The Irish Sons of Bitches did just that and had huge success in Japan in the 1990s. Their hits included 'Let's Burn A Union Jack', 'Give Us A Kiss Before I Pass Out' and 'If God Was Irish He'd Be As Drunk As A Fish'.

**5) The Guardians:** While a lot of Irish bands could be quite wild, The Guardians were more middle-of-the-road. In fact, their first album was called *MOR* and featured some fine songs, including 'I Love You', 'Blue Without You' and 'Too True For You'. Their second album, which was called *Less is MOR*, saw them go even more mainstream, with each song named after girls the band members had gone out with. Their biggest album, released in 1997, was called *More MOR AOR* and featured a lot of mature rock music designed for adults.

# 17
# TROUBLING TIMES

**We're all European Now**

As they were being denied access to many of the fun parts of the 1960s, the Irish kept their heads down, worked hard and prayed a lot, often getting to as many as nine Masses in a good week. Unfortunately, God didn't see fit to reward their abstinence with anything resembling improved economic prospects. After a relatively bright start to the decade, the bad times soon made an unwelcome return.

It didn't help that John F. Kennedy, the greatest Irishman ever, had been assassinated in 1963. He was a hero to most Irish people – and not just because of his incredible appetite for 'free love'. JFK represented the hope that the Irish could escape Ireland and get a good job in the US, preferably as president, though they would settle for working as a bent cop.

**The Promised Land**

However, that was not to be and Ireland had to look elsewhere for support. But where? South America? The USSR? SPECTRE? They were all possibilities, except for

**The Irish all became Europeans in 1973.**

the last one, which turned out to be a fictional global terrorist organisation invented by James Bond creator Ian Fleming. However, none really ticked all the boxes. The Irish were about to give up and resign themselves to a few more decades of recession, isolation and being nice to the English. Then, while out sailing below Cork one day, Taoiseach Jack Lynch spotted the continent and had a brilliant idea. 'Let's pretend we're part of that continent and join that EEC yoke.'

It was to be the beginning of a beautiful union. Ireland joined in 1973 and, more or less overnight, went from being wild Irish savages to sophisticated, modern Europeans. The future was getting bright, colourful and European, though it should be pointed out that the weather remained stubbornly dull, grey and Irish.

## Friends in the North

Unfortunately, things had become just a tad less than harmonious in the six counties of Northern Ireland. The border had apparently been drawn to ensure everyone got on together, but despite living very close to each other, the unionist and the nationalist communities didn't always get on all that spectacularly well. It wasn't long before the civil rights movement decided to get involved, but that didn't help either. In August 1969 the government in Westminster decided to send British Army troops into the North to help out, but not really surprisingly that just made matters worse.

This more or less marks the beginning of what are rather politely called The Troubles. It was a very clever name for the period as there really were plenty of troubles. Violence, sectarianism and name-calling were but the tip of the iceberg, as the six counties descended into decades of the worst kind of violence imaginable. It also included several Bloody Sundays, a couple of Bloody Fridays, various hunger strikes, a few marches and the rather unnecessary killing of innocent people. Just like any good, old-fashioned war really.

## Explaining the Troubles

Keeping track of the various factions during the Troubles was a difficult task for all concerned, not least those involved in it. Protagonists on both sides often had to ask people whose side they were on before shooting them. Then, when different groupings on the same side split into warring factions, things got even more confusing.

To help with this, the following is a simple guide to forty years of the Troubles: the IRA were republicans and hated the British Army, the RUC, the UDA and the UVF. The UDA were loyalists and hated the IRA, the INLA and the RUC, unless they happened to be working together on something. The INLA were republicans and they hated the UDA, but also hated the IRA, the UVF and the RUC. The UFF really hated the IRA, the INLA and the UDA, but were also really not keen on the UVF, who were hated by the Official IRA, though they hated everybody, but particularly the old RUC. The Provisional IRA also hated the UFF and the UVF, though they really hated the Official IRA. The UDA and the UVF, of course, hated each other, but not as much as they hated the IPLO, who were hated by both the RUC and the IRA. Now, this is where it gets confusing: the INLA hated the UVF, but not as much as the UVF hated them, though the UFF hated the new UDA more than they hated the old Provisional IRA. However, the new Real IRA really hated the Real UFF who in turn hated the old UFF, the Red Hand Defenders and the old Continuity IRA (and probably the new Continuity IRA).

When you've learned all those hatreds off, the situation in the North becomes a lot easier to understand.

## Peace Processes

With all those various organisations fighting each other, it was only a matter of time before peace was going to be achieved – a matter of a very long time. Of course, once politicians from the Republic, Britain and the US and anyone else who happened to be at a loose end also tried to help, things went from worse to even worser!

There were various attempts to force peace on the six counties, but all of them were eventually met with the most common word used by both sides from 1969 on: No! – as in 'Ulster Says No!' (although Ulster contains nine counties, not just the six in Northern Ireland), 'No Surrender!', 'No Chance!', 'No! No! No!' and 'Ach, did you not hear us saying "No!" the last few times?'

It wasn't until the Belfast Agreement of 1997 that people on both sides started saying 'Maybe!' instead of 'No!', though it has to be acknowledged that that took some effort on their part. If they could go from 'No!' to 'Maybe!', then there was hope that they might even stretch to a 'Yes!' one day.

## Family Affairs

The Troubles can be best represented by a well-known Belfast family called the Sweeneys. In 1948 a wholly holy Roman Catholic woman called Máire Sweeney married a staunch Protestant man called Billy Sweeney. Despite their extremely similar surnames, they were not related to each other in any way whatsoever. Except by marriage. They had two sons and two daughters, but despite that managed to live relatively happily together until 1969 when the Troubles really got going.

As religious and political divisions deepened, people were forced to take sides. Máire and the eldest boy, Seamus, and eldest girl, Caitlin, opted to support the republican side, while Billy and the second boy, Charles, and the youngest girl, Elizabeth, decided to back the unionists. This often led to fraught breakfasts, as tensions would rise between the two warring factions. It resulted in Máire and Billy having to ban all assault weapons from the kitchen just to keep the peace.

However, this wasn't enough and, in 1981, at the height of the republican hunger strikes, the Sweeneys erected a 'Peace Wall' wall down the middle of their small terraced house. When the Belfast Agreement was signed in 1997, Máire, Seamus and Elizabeth thought it was a good idea, while Billy, Charles and Caitlin were vehemently opposed to it. This led to renewed hostilities in the house, with Caitlin eventually splintering off on her own and forming the Real Sweeneys, a whole new family which she based in the living room. In response, Elizabeth set up the Continuity Red Hand Sweeneys and 'bordered' herself into the kitchen.

Meanwhile, Charles decided to get involved in petty criminal activities, which was a coincidence as Seamus had been hoping to get into that sort of stuff for the republican side since the late 1980s. They formed a successful partnership and always did things in a non-sectarian way, which made Billy and Máire very proud indeed. The family still live in their Belfast home and only really fight around St Patrick's Day and at the height of the marching season in July.

# Top Five

## Radio Shows That May Still Be Broadcasting

Ireland has always been known as a nation of talkers, from traditional sean-nós storytellers through to that guy at the end of the bar who won't shut up and swears he met your Aunt Carmel at a hooley in Ballybofey on a rainy Friday in June 1956. This propensity for chat has transferred to the more modern medium of radio, on which people get to bask in the sound of their own voices. Here are five of the most popular Irish radio shows of all time, some of which may even be broadcasting as you read this:

1) **Talking Shop:** The longest-running radio programme in world history, 'Talking Shop' has been on the air since even before the invention of radio. It runs 24 hours a day, seven days a week and has no host. Basically, if there is something you're not happy about, you just phone up and start complaining. All callers get to have their voices heard, so there could be as many as two or three thousand people talking over each other at any given moment. If you listen long enough, the sound turns into a sort of sleep-inducing hum.

2) **Desperate Dan's Daily Dose:** Dan McCurtain's radio show, which apparently goes out between 1 a.m. and 4 a.m. every morning, features phone interviews with some of the nastiest members of society. Often phoning from their basements or dungeons, these people are given a voice by the radical McCurtain because he believes 'everyone has a right to be heard' and 'it helps my ratings'. However, the Garda Síochána disagree and generally track down and arrest anyone who phones the show, often without even bothering to hear what they have to say.

**3) Mass Appeal – The One True Show:** Christian radio is a big thing all over the world and this is no less true in Ireland. The 'Mass Appeal' show is on national radio from 8 a.m. to 12.01 p.m. every day and includes three Masses, a selection of pithy songs about Jesus, various people talking about how they found, lost and then found their faith again and the Angelus. However, it is not all serious and the show will often feature more light-hearted segments, including 'The Singing Priest Half-Hour', 'Miracles For All The Family' and 'Pets In Heaven'.

**4) The Past In The Present:** They say that the past is a foreign country, but from 5 a.m. to 7 a.m. every morning, it isn't a foreign country at all, but Ireland. Listeners to the 'The Past In The Present' are urged to phone in and recite poems they wrote when they were four, sing songs they learned while still in crèche and even do the odd dance or jig. The chat is interspersed with various bits of traditional Irish music, though it was recently discovered that they had actually been playing the same piece of music over and over again since 1924. The beauty of it was that no one noticed.

**5) Christmas On The Radio:** Everyone loves a good Christmas song, as well as information about what presents to buy for your loved ones and where. However, it is often hard to find this information in the months from January to August when a lot of people try not to think about Christmas. This show, which has its own dedicated channel, fills that niche gap, as it is only broadcast during those months. So if you want to know where to buy nice socks and hear 'Jingle Bells', 'I Saw Mommy Kissing Santa Claus' and 'Fairytale of New York' while you're at the beach, this is for you.

# 18
# BRAVE NEW IRELAND

**The Irish even started to dress like Europeans.**

### A Place in the Sun

Despite the Troubles, the Republic decided to try to lead as normal a life as possible in the 1970s and 1980s. This often involved telling white lies about its neighbour, such as 'Fighting? In the North? Haven't heard any!' or 'Northern Ireland? No, that's in the Middle East.'

Joining the EEC was also a good idea as it gave the Republic access to new markets, some much needed sunshine and European cash. To this end, the Irish government issued strict guidelines to all Irish citizens in a 1974 document called *The Poor Mouth: Getting the Most out of Europe*. It instructed Irish people on how to behave if they met Europeans from other EEC member states. This included saying how just a few quid would sort the whole country out and that Ireland needed more roads. The Irish were also keen to trade with their new business partners and were happy to exchange butter mountains, milk lakes and potato piles for wine, pizza and bucket-loads of tiramisu.

## Mass Opposition

While joining the EEC might have made sense for the economic well-being of the nation, there was something much more important at stake: the very soul of the nation. Ireland had always been the most devout country in all of Christendom, but would being more closely linked to foreign types damage the country? It was hard not to see this happening, as everyone knew what the French, Italians and Spanish were like. The Danes and Swedes also had notoriously dodgy morals which were bound to rub off on the Irish if given half a chance.

The Catholic Church did all it could to prevent this, including forbidding all Scandinavians from entering

Ireland, banning the Irish from travelling abroad and threatening to tell God if any Irish person was found staring at tanned, good-looking foreigners. However, in reality there was little that could be done to stop the flood of immorality and the Church's influence started to wane. Irish people would huddle around their illegal TV sets in the 1980s, watching glamorous foreign programmes such as *Dallas*, *Coronation Street* and *The Benny Hill Show* and dreaming of a better life.

## Fighting for a Different Kind of Freedom

When the state finally went against the Church's wishes and made TV legal in 1983, it was all over bar the shouting, the sighing and the soft, gentle moaning: Ireland's soul was lost. Women were allowed to think for themselves and could wear underwear that hadn't been issued by the Church. It was discovered that things like divorce, contraception and homosexuality weren't quite as evil as people had been told and didn't make bits of your body fall off. Men and women began to indulge in all sorts of immoral horseplay – and often with each other.

The Church's grip was further loosened when it was discovered that the moral fibre of some of their 'spiritual guardians' in the Church was, to say the least, criminally lax. The scandals that beset the Church not only shocked Irish people; even God was quite upset about it.

The Irish left the Church in their thousands. One shocking statistic reveals that between 1991 and 2006, the percentage of Ireland's population who said they were Catholic dropped from 92 per cent to just 6 per cent. (Note: that second figure was actually 86 per cent, not 6 per cent. It was changed during the editing process to make the drop seem more dramatic. This is called artistic licence.)

## Ups and Downs, Ins and Outs

Although times had been better for Ireland since it joined the EEC, the 1980s weren't looking great. However, a new leader had emerged in the late 1970s, a leader for whom a country's economic issues were unimportant, especially when compared to his own. A direct descendant of St Patrick and Brian Boru, his name was Charles J. Haughey, leader of Fianna Fáil, and he was Taoiseach more than seventy times during the decade. Each time he became leader, things seemed to get better for everybody, though really just for him.

It seemed that Haughey was hoping that there would be some nice chap out there who would pick up the pieces after he left office. And he was right: this particular chap's name was Garret FitzGerald, leader of Fine Gael, who alternated holding the office of Taoiseach with Haughey throughout the 1980s. Whenever people discovered what Haughey was up to and how he was ruining the country, he would be booted out. FitzGerald would come in and clean up the mess by inflicting as much economic pain as possible on everyone. Once that was done, Fianna Fáil would get back in again. This meant the country could continue its long and not very glorious history of being broke.

Haughey was later discredited and the Irish swore they would never fall for those kinds of tricks again – or not for a few years at least.

**Taoiseach Charles Haughey urged people to cut back while he cut loose.**

## Getting Nifty in the 1990s

Despite all this, the Irish economy was starting to improve as the 1980s drew to a close. Economists have sought many causes for this gradual change, citing Ireland's low corporation tax, some crucial fiscal correction and various other technical, academic and, to be honest, rather boring reasons.

Most ordinary people know that the reason for the improved finances was the fact that Ireland won the World Cup in 1990, though some records of the time allege that Ireland actually lost in the quarter-finals of Italia '90. Having first achieved success under new manager Jack Charlton at the European Championships in 1988, where they beat England 1–0, Ireland would go on to win their first tournament at Italia '90. Charlton, who was about as Irish as somebody who wasn't Irish, selected the team himself, often happy to use Irish players if there were no eligible English ones left. Whatever their nationality, the national team was supported by the whole nation and this time Ireland beat England 1–1. Incredibly, this sporting victory was followed by Ireland winning the Eurovision Song Contest an unbelievable nineteen times between 1990 and 2000.

The victories led to a new sense of optimism in Ireland, a new self-confidence, a new belief that the days of being oppressed by the English, the Church or anybody else were over and that a new Ireland would now arise. And this new Ireland would be strong, powerful and confident and the world would hear its roar, the roar of a never-ending economic boom, the roar of a tiger.

## The Spy Who Stayed Out in the Cold

The Cold War escalated in the 1980s as the world's two most super superpowers developed nuclear weapons and realised they could now annihilate their enemy (and the rest of the planet while they were at it). The two warring empires were the US of A in the blue corner, representing freedom, apple pie and all the good stuff, and the USSR in the red corner, representing oppression, borscht and all the bad stuff.

Most countries had to choose which side to be on, though Ireland was pretty much forced to choose the US side and even had to send spies on behalf of the US to live in the USSR. The most famous of these was Kim Sweeneykov, who coincidentally and rather fortunately had a Russian surname. He lived in Moscow from 1976 to 1984 and collected information that he was supposed to pass back to his handler in G2, the Irish spy agency. The only problem with this was that Kim was, due to serious staff shortages, also his own handler.

This meant that he kept all the information to himself, particularly the stuff about nuclear power. When he returned to Ireland at the end of the Cold War, he was given a local government grant to use his knowledge to develop nuclear power as an alternative to fossil fuels. However, some sort of mix-up occurred, and Kim used his research to build nuclear weapons instead. He built 150 warheads between 1992 and 2002 and hid them in locations around Ireland.

In the last ten years, Kim began selling these warheads off to whoever wanted one, though he point-blank refused to sell to children, unless they had the cash upfront. It is believed he still has more than sixty for sale, though he says that at this stage of his life, he might just use them himself. Irish people live under this constant threat, though Kim isn't too worried as he lives on his own island in the Caribbean.

# Top Five

## Irish TV Shows That Nearly Wowed the World

The Irish came to television late, but when they started making their own shows there was no stopping them – though people frequently tried. Some of the best shows made in the country included *The News*, *Celebrity Farm* and *The Angelus*, but there were others that were slightly smaller hits.

1) **Killybacon:** This farm-based soap opera featured the trials and tribulations of a large rural family, a big herd of cows and a sheep. One reason for its success was that all of the actors, including the animals, played themselves. Cameras filmed the family twenty-four hours a day, seven days a week, with those 168 hours of footage then edited down to one very interesting half-hour.

2) **Stampo:** The most popular kids show ever on Irish TV was hosted by a hand-puppet called Stampo. He showed cartoons and told jokes to all the young children invited onto the show. Despite its huge popularity, it only ran for one episode, as Stampo was arrested on unspecified charges. However, as

he was only a puppet, he managed to avoid trial on a technicality. Stampo emigrated soon after and currently lives in relative obscurity in Thailand.

**3) Farmers' Fabulous Wives:** Broadcast from 1985 to 1998, this was the world's first quiz to exclusively feature the wives of farmers. Hosted by the extremely charming Dash White, the wives had to answer a series of questions related to farming by choosing from various special categories, which included Hearty Breakfasts, Combine Harvesters, Lambing and Immanuel Kant's *Critique of Pure Reason*.

**4) The Show of Chat:** The chat show reached its apex in this programme, which was Ireland's most watched show for thirty years. Hosted by the outspoken Sr Fidelma Bracken, the show was famous for confronting big issues. These included one shocking programme in which a couple revealed that they had actually enjoyed kissing. Naturally, Catholic priests frowned upon this, as kissing or rather the prevention thereof, was their gig. They went on the show the following Friday to condemn kissing, but by that stage no one was tuning in.

**5) Dub Town:** It was only a matter of time before someone came up with a gritty soap opera set in one of Dublin's rougher areas. The controversial 'Dub Town' took urban drama to places it had been scared to go to before and each episode showed shootings, cars being burnt out and several of the main characters dying from drug overdoses. It was very popular, but ended after just two years when it was revealed that a lot of the footage was real.

# 19

# THE ROAR OF
# THE TIGER

## Before the Roar

Since the extinction of the dinosaurs just over 65
million years ago, Ireland had never enjoyed two years
in a row where the economy had done well. Recession
had followed recession, which had generally come
just after another recession. Then there might be two
weeks of growth before another recession kicked in.
This memorably happened in the years 640 BCE, 876
CE and 1822.

Added to this, the much put-upon Gaels had also
had their fair share of non-recessionary bad luck,
including being located right next to a country which
was very keen on colonising other countries. The Irish
had been oppressed, suppressed and repressed to
within an inch of their lives – and often further. Even
those who were supposed to help them, such as the
clergy, the politicians and the Department of Social
Welfare, often treated the ordinary folk rather poorly.
Through it all, the Irish kept on laughing, drinking,

singing and making fun of the English. But maybe they also knew down deep that, sooner or later, they would have their day in the sun – although it was unlikely to be literally 'in the sun'.

## Green Shoots

From the 1990s on, things began to pick up for Ireland, but it was only when Ireland changed its official status at the UN from 'nation' to 'economy' that things started to really improve. Being a nation was all well and good, but an economy was all about the money.

Various initiatives were introduced which, it was hoped, would kick-start the economy. For a start, every

Irish citizen was ordered by the government to buy at least four houses. If they claimed not to have enough money, the government rather forcibly suggested that they borrow it from a friend or from a bank, which was kind of like a friend.

This created a huge demand for houses, which had to be built all over the country, including in places where no one really wanted to live, such as in bogs, under motorway bridges and in the rather scarily named 'ghost' estates. This led to a boom for the construction industry and saw developers, estate agents and banks all get very rich. As the banks were so rich, they very kindly decided to lend the people more money they didn't want to buy more stuff they didn't need. And with everyone buying stuff on credit, nothing could go wrong, as the money didn't really exist in the first place.

The Irish were also lucky to have some dependable financial institutions to look after everything on their behalf. The people knew that no matter what happened, their banks and their government would always look out for their best interests.

## Winning the Euromillions

As things were starting to get better, the Irish then made another shrewd financial decision: they would use German money for all future transactions. After all, the Germans had tried to conquer Europe twice and failed; if they tried again, they might just succeed and Ireland didn't want to miss out on that.

Using Germany's currency, or the 'euro' as it became known, was achieved by becoming part of the Eurozone, which came into being on 1 January 1999. The creation of the euro was perfect for Ireland, as it ensured that its financial health was intrinsically linked to Germany and the other big nations of the EU. Again, it was a vital safety net if anything ever went wrong. Not that it would.

## Soldiers of Great Fortune

The political party overseeing all this wealth creation was Fianna Fáil, which had cleverly changed its name from 'Soldiers of Destiny' to 'Soldiers of Fortune'. Bertie Ahern, probably the chattiest Taoiseach in history, led it. His genius as a politician was that he kept talking and talking until people got bored and agreed with him.

The economic growth also helped to boost the country's image abroad and suddenly every multinational in the world wanted to have their European headquarters in Ireland. This, in turn, inspired millions of others to establish their own technology firms based on the fact that the Internet was quite big and seemed to be getting bigger all the time.

Tourists flocked to the country to see just how rich everyone was. Bus tours around wealthy areas were very popular, and tourists gazed in wonder as they passed by gleaming new office buildings, stunning apartment blocks and glamorous housing estates.

The golden rule of capitalism states that everything is working fine as long as the rich keep getting richer, but this was even better: it wasn't just the rich getting richer, as even poor people were now rolling in it.

This perfect economic miracle was christened the Celtic Tiger, as it was a powerful, hungry beast which would devour anything in its path and which could not be stopped.

## The Tiger's Roar

It was a great time to be Irish. The country became the envy of the world, as every other nation tried to emulate the miracle of building an economy on the very stable foundation of mass credit. Ireland also became a proper modern nation, with mature problems the citizens could be proud of, such as racism and organised crime.

Unemployment dropped down to about minus 20 per cent, with most people actually having four or five very well-paid jobs. They also played the stock market at night and looked after their property portfolios while flying their helicopters to their third or fourth homes.

The situation became so bizarre that even people who had previously refused to work signed off the dole and got jobs, albeit jobs that often involved sitting around doing nothing, except maybe calling in sick on Mondays and Fridays. Still, even that was a skill much in demand during the Celtic Tiger years.

## Living the High Life

The standard of living also surged dramatically, particularly between 2000 and 2007. Most Irish people owned three or four sports cars, a private jet and at least ten racehorses and survived on a rather slimming diet of truffles, champagne and cocaine.

The Celtic Tiger brought success to the Irish as

never before, although the most important thing about it was not the fact that everyone had gotten rich so quickly, but that it was a long-term, sustainable, never-ending economic boom which would see the Irish continue to be wealthy forever and ever.

## The Best St Patrick's Day Ever!

Since pretty much the beginning of time, the Irish used to get together on St Patrick's Day to discuss what it meant to be Irish and whether it was a good thing or not. In the past, this would have often been a quiet affair, with just a few important people meeting in the local pub. Later, this grew into a bigger affair, at which songs about freedom would be sung and a small glass or two raised to Irishness. Later, they used to throw in the odd parade, which usually featured tractors, sheep that been painted green and some majorettes from the US who had been told they were Irish and therefore had to walk along an Irish street in the cold as punishment.

However, the Celtic Tiger changed all that and St Patrick's Day gradually became a week-long festival that celebrated all that was great about being Irish. This reached its apex in the now infamous St Patrick's Day Month-Long World Festival of Irish Greatness in 2007, which was organised by Atticus 'Paddy' O'Sweeney, one of the O'Sweeneys of East Donegal, The Bronx and, more recently, San Quentin State Prison.

For the occasion, Paddy ordered four million bottles of 'green' Champagne from France, had any river that wasn't already greenish dyed green and presented every Irish citizen with an emerald brooch, a green Mercedes-Benz and one of those tartan-hat-red-wig combos. It was widely recognised as the biggest party ever held on the planet. Billions of people from all over the world joined in, all claiming to be Irish or, at the very least, to have snogged someone who might once have claimed to be Irish.

When it was later discovered that the Celtic Tiger economic miracle hadn't really been that miraculous or Celtic, the state went after Paddy to try to recoup the €24 billion he had spent on the festival. Unfortunately, he was feeling quite ill that day and wasn't up for talking about it. In fact, his doctor had recommended that he leave Ireland immediately and go to live somewhere warm, sunny and quite far away.

The Irish government then secretly added the bill for the festival to all of Ireland's other debts and hoped no one would notice, as the overall figures were so huge and meaningless anyway. So far, they've gotten away with it and it now looks unlikely the Irish people will ever find out.

# Top Five

## Irish Myths That Might Actually Be True

As most people now know, the period of economic growth known as the Celtic Tiger turned out to be a bit of a myth, but it is not the only popular one in Irish history. From the Blarney Stone and children who were actually swans to a singing shamrock and the song 'You'll Never Beat The Irish', the country has had more than its fair share of legends.

1) **Leprechauns:** These impertinent little fellows, who look like a cross between tall, ugly fairies and small, ugly men, are magical creatures that drink too much, talk too much and wear way too much green. The trickiest thing about leprechauns is that they are both notorious liars and invisible, so if you meet one and ask him if he's really there, you just can't believe his answer.

2) **Fairies:** Irish fairies are not quite the small, gentle beings you come across in the mythology of other countries. They are a bit more vicious and mean and don't like dancing, singing or being called Tinkerbell. In fact, they are more like the elves in *The Lord of the Rings*, though with very bad hangovers.

**Banshee wailing was made illegal in 2006.**

**3) Banshees:** These creatures generally take the form of
old hags, though sometimes they can look like
beautiful young women, so be careful if you're
out on the town looking for action. If you hear a
banshee wailing, there's a good chance you might
be dying – or, in the worst case scenario, you may
already be dead. Banshees' screams tend to be very
annoying and were outlawed by the Environmental

Protection Agency in 2006, though banshees think of themselves as being above the law, so they haven't stopped.

**4) The Talking Potato of Lisganagh:** The Talking Potato of Lisganagh is still probably Ireland's most famous talking vegetable (apart, perhaps, from The Chatty Turnip of Tullystown). It used to predict all sorts of things, such as the weather, and even the exact start date of the First World War, though it didn't do that until 1917. Discredited in recent years after an affair with a carrot, the Talking Potato is rarely seen in public nowadays and is said to be working on an autobiography entitled *When the Chips are Down*.

**5) The Everlasting Pint of Ardnablona:** Controversy still surrounds the Everlasting Pint, as many swear it's true and that it is hiding in a cave near Galway. No matter how many times you drain the glass, it simply fills back up again with the sweetest stout you have ever tasted. It is now a major tourist attraction, though the locals also try to make it out to the cave in Ardnablona whenever they have a spare moment. Be warned, though, that the queue hasn't been shorter than four kilometres since the War of Independence.

# 20

# THE RISE AND FALL AND RISE OF THE IRISH EMPIRE

Some nice rich folk decided it would be best if the poor paid for the global recession.

## Death of a Wild Animal

In a bizarre twist which no one saw coming, Ireland's never-ending boom ended. One day there was lots of credit, good will and expensive property knocking around. The next day everyone was broke. The banks collapsed, the government collapsed and eventually most Irish people collapsed too.

Around the world, economies went into recession at a rate of 300 or 400 a day. It was also discovered that the main cause for the worldwide recession was a technical and little-known term related to macroeconomics, global finances and free market capitalism called 'greed'. This 'greed' thing had apparently driven a lot of developers, banks, financial institutions, investors and stockbrokers to try to make as much money as possible in as short a space of time as possible. To do this they had used every trick in the book, as well as some tricks that weren't in the book for fairly obvious reasons.

As the economic miracle came crashing down, it became clear that someone was going to have to pay. So all the groups involved got together to discuss the issue. Unfortunately, there wasn't enough space in the room to fit all the millions of citizens, so they had to trust the others to make the right decision. Unfortunately, the decision went against the citizens and it was decided that they should be the ones to pay.

For the Irish, this meant they had to sell their sovereignty to the highest bidder, which turned out to be three international money-lenders, collectively known as The Troika. Irish sovereignty was only worth a few quid and the Irish people were left with a debt which was estimated to be somewhere between €243 billion and €897 billion. When the Irish tried to get an exact figure, they were told that it was so huge that it didn't really matter and that they should let their great-great-great-great-great-great-grandchildren worry about it.

## The Wasteland

Life in Ireland after the collapse of the economy was not much fun and reminded people of a great potato famine or of being oppressed by a foreign power, which coincidentally were the two things Irish people hated most. Unemployment grew to levels not seen since the Battle of Clontarf ended in 1014 and emigration yet again appeared to be the best solution. People left the country in their droves, seeking a better life or at least one that didn't involve paying back other people's massive gambling debts.

From 2008 onwards people just got more and more miserable, as the powers-that-be inflicted austerity on the Irish. This basically meant that people had to pay for every single thing going, including taking a walk in the park, breathing air and staring at anything that was owned by the state. If you were lucky enough to have a job, you had to work four times the hours you were doing previously for a quarter of the pay. Not only that, but each morning you had to go to your boss, get down on your knees and thank them for increasing your hours and cutting your wages. Then, at the end of the week, you had to bring your entire salary around to the government who very kindly sent it to Europe, which they also charged you for.

The Fianna Fáil-led government had actually come up with a plan to save the country called the Programme for Pain, but it wasn't particularly popular. Then Fine Gael and the Labour Party formed a coalition that offered new hope for the future. They came up with a plan to save the country, which they called the Programme for Hope. Unfortunately, it was discovered later that it was the same document Fianna Fáil had used, but with the word 'Pain' crossed out and the word 'Hope' written on the cover in black crayon instead.

### The Future of History

The recession in Ireland began to ease in 2014 and there was hope that things would keep getting better and better. Property prices rose, unemployment fell and consumers consumed again. The construction sector, in particular, was starting to see some action, which is always a good sign in an economy. In fact, it wasn't forgotten that it had heralded great things to come in the years leading up to the Celtic Tiger.

**The Irish had learned their lesson with Tiger One.**

It had been a tough few years, but everyone in Ireland was looking forward to an improvement in their fortunes. They were particularly hopeful that the value of their houses would get back up to those dangerously high Celtic Tiger levels.

More importantly, as the economy improved, people were desperately searching for a name to give to an economy that had boomed and bust so spectacularly and then started to grow again. There were a lot of arguments about this in pubs at night, as it was so important to get the name right. No one wanted to come up with a name that would curse Ireland to repeat the mistakes of the past.

Finally, in a referendum held in March 2015, a name was chosen, a name which would show that Ireland's economy was a powerful, hungry beast which would devour anything in its path and which could never be stopped: Tiger Two. The future of Irish history was getting boomier, roarier and brighter all over again. (Note: two of those aren't even real words.)

## When the Going Gets Tough

In the years after the Great Crash of 2008, the Irish landscape could, at best, have been described as a post-apocalyptic wilderness. There were abandoned cars, empty apartment buildings, overgrown 'ghost' estates, wild dogs running loose and zombies attacking the few remaining survivors. (Note: that last part about zombies may not be 100 per cent historically accurate, but was added to make history seem more interesting.) It was hard for anyone to survive, let alone make a few quid.

However, one enterprising young man did – and not only that but he managed to help others while he was at it. His name was Vincent 'Honest Vinny' Sweeney of the Cricklewood and Cayman Island Sweeneys. In the boom years, he ran his own 'charity' called Sweeney Developments, which built housing for the needy, though as Vinny himself said: 'Everyone is "needy" in a property bubble.'

However, when the recession hit, Vinny lost billions of euros, though fortunately it was mainly other people's money. He lost a few quid himself, but not the millions he had lodged in his four-year-old daughter's Cayman Island accounts. A lot of developers had high-tailed it out of Ireland when things got bad, but Vinny was one of the more honest ones, hence the name 'Honest Vinny'. He told the Irish government he would look after some of the nicer properties it had on its books after other developers had defaulted on loans. Vinny did this for a small fee and even managed to sell a few of the properties for the country, albeit at knockdown prices. But as Vinny himself said: 'Beggars can't be choosers when a bubble bursts.'

Of course, the great thing for Vinny was that the

economy started to pick up again, so whoever bought those properties from him may have got themselves a bargain. And maybe the new owner, which seems to be a shelf company called Sweeney Shelving Ltd which is run by a four-year-old girl and based in the Cayman Islands, will hire the newly resurgent Sweeney Developments to build even more properties. It would be nice for Vinny to get some reward for helping Ireland out in its time of need.

# Top Five

## Reasons Why the World Will Never Forget Ireland

As most people know, the main difference between the past and the future is that one has pretty much already happened, while the other is going to happen – and probably very soon. So, while it is all well and good to write a 'trueish' history of Ireland, it is perhaps even more important to look at its 'trueish' future – though it would be very hard to fill a whole book with it. Here are five reasons why Ireland and the Irish will stay in people's hearts and minds long into its trueish future:

1) **It's Little and Great:** Often described as a 'great little country', Ireland is indeed a very nice place. The

weather isn't great and it seems to lurch from utter poverty to startling wealth in a remarkably consistent cycle, but despite this, it is a beautiful place full of wonderfully friendly folk. And while most people probably wouldn't want to live on the island, many are only too happy to visit every few years. They come and soak up the atmosphere, the rain, the potatoes and as many pints of stout as they can.

2) **The Gift of the Gab:** If there is one thing that people seem to like about Ireland more than any other, it is the Irish. Having been here for an awfully long time, it is safe to state that the Irish are now more Irish than the Irish themselves – or anybody else for that matter. Friendly, upbeat and chatty, you'll never beat the Irish when it comes to looking on the bright side of life. The gift of the gab, which you can either order online or get by kissing the Blarney Stone in Cork, ensures the Irish will always have the right word to make others happy. And if others are happy, then so are the Irish.

3) **St Patrick's Day:** There are very few national days that are celebrated globally, but somehow St Patrick's Day has become a massive day out all over the known world – and possibly even further afield.

Whether you have Irish roots or not, 17 March is a chance to let your hair down and be 'Irish' for the day – or at least until closing time. It's also an opportunity to have a few drinks and, if you're lucky, convince people to kiss you merely because you're Irish, drunk or both. To be fair, on St Patrick's Day, most people are Irish whether you kiss them or not.

**4) The Irish Are Everywhere:** Another reason why the Irish will endure in the global consciousness is that nearly sixty per cent of the world's population claim to be of Irish descent. That's well over four billion people – though it is estimated to rise as high as five billion on St Patrick's Day. That's a very large number of people by anyone's calculations. Of course, while the Irish are proud of this diaspora, they wouldn't want them all to come 'home' at the same time, even if it was for a short visit. Still, postcards or envelopes containing cash are generally welcomed.

**5) The True(ish) Future of Ireland:** Most importantly, the future for Ireland is looking very bright indeed, though that could just be a break in the clouds. This means that one day someone will have to write a book called *The True(ish) Future of Ireland*, which will ensure that the country will never be forgotten. The Irish are also very worried about your future which is why they may give you this blessing if they meet you down the pub: 'May your glass be ever full, May the roof over your head be always strong, And may you be in Heaven half an hour before the devil knows you're dead.' Which, when you think about it, is all any of us want ...

## MERCIER PRESS

IRISH PUBLISHER - IRISH STORY

We hope you enjoyed this book.

Since 1944, Mercier Press has published books that have been critically important to Irish life and culture.

Our website is the best place to find out more information about Mercier, our books, authors, news and the best deals on a wide variety of books. Mercier tracks the best prices for our books online and we seek to offer the best value to our customers, offering free delivery within Ireland.

A large selection of Mercier's new releases and backlist are also available as ebooks. We have an ebook for everyone, with titles available for the Amazon Kindle, Sony Reader, Kobo Reader, Apple products and many more. Visit our website to find and buy our ebooks.

Sign up on our website to receive updates and special offers.

www.mercierpress.ie
www.facebook.com/mercier.press
www.twitter.com/irishpublisher